MW00472798

Josephus's *The Jewish War*

Josephus's *The Jewish War*

A BIOGRAPHY

Martin Goodman

PRINCETON UNIVERSITY PRESS

Princeton and Oxford

Copyright © 2019 by Princeton University Press

Published by Princeton University Press
41 William Street, Princeton, New Jersey 08540
6 Oxford Street, Woodstock, Oxfordshire OX20 1TR

press.princeton.edu

All Rights Reserved

Library of Congress Control Number: 2019937985
ISBN 978-0-691-13739-1
ISBN (e-book) 978-0-691-19419-6

British Library Cataloging-in-Publication Data is available

Editorial: Fred Appel, Thalia Leaf and Jenny Tan
Production Editorial: Jenny Wolkowicki
Text design: Lorraine Doneker
Jacket design: Lorraine Doneker
Production: Erin Suydam
Publicity: Nathalie Levine and Kathryn Stevens
Copyeditor: Joseph Dahm

Jacket credit: The Arch of Titus, depicting the Spoils of Jerusalem.
Constructed in c. 82 AD by the emperor Domitian to commemorate
Titus's victories. Lanmas / Alamy

This book has been composed in Garamond Premier Pro

Printed on acid-free paper. ∞

Printed in the United States of America

10 9 8 7 6 5 4 3 2 1

CONTENTS

In many Jewish and Christian homes in England or America in the nineteenth century, a beautifully bound copy of William Whiston's translation of Josephus could be found on the shelf next to a copy of the Bible. The name of the author was sufficiently recognized for casual allusions to be dropped into the writings of Mark Twain and Thomas Hardy. The writings of Josephus were included in the select library of forty works donated to the Collegiate School of Connecticut on the foundation of what was to become Yale University. It was widely known that he had described the fall of Jerusalem to the Romans in the *Jewish War*. How many owners of these bound volumes found their way actually to read what Josephus wrote is another question.

The life of the *Jewish War* will include not only the copying, printing, distribution, editing, translating, and adapting of Josephus's history, but also fluctuations in the reputation of the author and his book over two thousand years. In the modern world, attitudes toward the *Jewish War* are deeply ambivalent, with some passages, such as the description of the defense of Masada, treated as if they were eyewitness reportage (even though Josephus was not there) and others, such as the account of Titus's council of war before the destruction of the Jerusalem Temple, often dismissed as imperial propaganda (even though, according to his own account, Josephus was in the Roman military headquarters at the time and in a position to know what actually happened). Attitudes toward the *Jewish War* have owed as much to the changing fortunes of Jews in the centuries after the book was completed as they do to the contents of the work itself. But Josephus's history was a remarkable work in its own right— and, as we shall see, at least occasionally it was actually read.

This biography owes its birth to Fred Appel in Princeton University Press, on whose initiative Josephus's *Jewish War* has been included in the Princeton *Lives of Great Religious Books* series. It was not an obvious choice, since the *Jewish War* was not in origin a sacred text, but it was inspired, since investigation into its reception has been bound up in the developments of both Judaism and Christianity since antiquity. The story culminates in the passionate debates about Josephus and his book among Jews since the early nineteenth century. My extended treatment of this topic in chapter 4 reflects both the interest of these debates and their reverberations to the present day.

Reception history benefits hugely from collaboration, since no one scholar can hope to know everything about the disparate cultures within which a book has been passed down and read over the centuries, and I have been exceptionally fortunate to have benefited from the wisdom and knowledge of a wide range of colleagues. In 2014 the Oxford Seminar in Advanced Jewish Studies at the Centre for Hebrew and Jewish Studies brought together a galaxy of scholars over six months to investigate the reception of Josephus in the early modern period. Between 2012 and 2015 a research project funded by the Arts and Humanities Research Council convened four workshops in Oxford to study the Jewish reception of Josephus from 1750 to the present. I am deeply grateful to Joanna Weinberg, my colleague in leading the Oxford Seminar, and to Tessa Rajak and Andrea Schatz, who were co-investigators on the AHRC project, as well as to the many scholars (more than fifty) who contributed their knowledge to the sessions organized under the auspices of one or another of these immensely valuable collaborative ventures. Panel discussions at the conferences of the Association of Jewish Studies, the World Union of Jewish Studies, and the European Association of Jewish Studies, and responses to a conference presentation at Johns Hopkins University, elicited yet more ideas. It has been exhilarating to discover how many colleagues, with expertise from antiquity to the present, have proven to have discovered at least one curious reference to Josephus in the material they study.

I am much indebted to Anthony Ellis, Theofili Kampianaki, Tessa Rajak, Daniel Schwartz, and Joanna Weinberg for reading earlier drafts of this book and providing immensely helpful comments. They have saved me from many errors. Any that remain are my responsibility alone.

My acquaintance with Josephus's original text has been greatly enriched by working with Martin Hammond on the Oxford World's Classics edition, published by Oxford University Press in 2017, and I am very grateful to him for permission to use his translation in the passages cited in the appendix. I am also very grateful to Zur Shalev and Eyal Ben Eliyahu for permission to quote the translation of 'Josephus' by Yitzhak Shalev, and to Neelum Ali for her patience in turning my handwriting into typescript.

LIVES OF GREAT RELIGIOUS BOOKS

Josephus's *The Jewish War*

Beginnings

CHAPTER I

Josephus the Man

Josephus began his life as a scion of a priestly Jewish family in Judaea and ended it, probably in Rome, as a Roman citizen who could boast a personal acquaintance with at least two emperors. The vicissitudes of his career can be attributed directly to the revolt of the Jews against Roman rule that culminated in the destruction of Jerusalem and its famous Temple in 70 CE. That conflict was the subject of the *Jewish War*, and the story of the course and aftermath of the war will overshadow every page of this account of his most famous book.

Josephus was born in 37 CE and raised in Jerusalem. His paternal ancestors were priests, and he could trace his lineage back to a great-great-grandmother who had been a Hasmonean princess in the late second century BCE. The family was prominent in Judaean society, and Josephus as a child witnessed upheavals in the fortunes of the city. He was four in 41 CE when Agrippa I, grandson of Herod the Great, was appointed king of Judaea by the Roman emperor Claudius, and seven when Agrippa suddenly died, 'eaten up by worms', after he had appeared in public dressed so gorgeously in a silver robe that he appeared to some to be presenting himself as divine. For the next twenty-two years Judaea was ruled directly by Roman governors. Agrippa II, Agrippa's son, was deemed by the emperor too young to become king in Judaea, but both he and his family retained close ties to the levers of power in Judaean politics. In 46 CE the governor appointed was Tiberius Julius Alexander, scion of an aristocratic Jewish family from Alexandria in Egypt whose brother had once been married to Agrippa II's sister Berenice, and from ca. 50 CE Agrippa II himself was given the task of administering the Temple that dominated the social and economic life of Jerusalem. Josephus had close links with all three of these influential Jews, who were to loom large in the conflict with Rome that erupted in 66 CE.[1]

By his twenties Josephus was sufficiently prominent in the politics of Jerusalem to go on an embassy to Rome in ca. 62 CE to plead for the release of some priests who had been sent there as prisoners. The issue that had led to their captivity is unknown, but it is clear that he was deeply enmeshed in the fighting within the Judaean elite for influence that plagued Judaea during the fifties CE, and he was present in the Temple in 66 CE when a faction of the priestly elite marked rebellion from Roman rule by ending the ancient custom of offering a sacrifice to the Jewish God for the well-being of the emperor (2.409). The initial attempts by Rome to reimpose order were unsuccessful, and in October 66 the government of the self-declared independent Jewish state appointed Josephus to oversee the defense of Galilee against the expected Roman assault.

In the *Jewish War* (2.563–3.411, 432–42), Josephus described his career as a general in Galilee in heroic terms, but the result was failure. In the early months of 67 the newly appointed Roman general Vespasian subdued the region by compelling the Jewish forces to take refuge in hilltop settlements that were then systematically besieged, and the siege of Jotapata ended with the capture of Josephus himself.

Capture by Vespasian had profound consequences for the rest of Josephus's life. According to his own account, he had made a suicide pact with the comrades with whom he found himself trapped in a cave, but when only he and one other remained alive he was divinely inspired to break the pact and surrender to the Romans. When hauled before Vespasian and his son Titus, Josephus was similarly inspired to prophesy that Vespasian would become emperor (3.399–408). At the time the prophecy was deeply implausible, since Vespasian came from quite a humble background, but in June 69, in a year of civil turmoil throughout the Roman world during which four emperors came to power in turn, Vespasian made a bid for supreme power and Josephus's prophecy came true. In Suetonius's biography of Vespasian, written in the early second century, it is for this prophecy that Josephus is remembered.[2]

The story of the prophecy may be doubted since it was in the interest of both Josephus and Vespasian to claim that Vespasian's rise to power had been divinely predicted. But the story was enough to ensure that in the summer of 69 Josephus was released from captivity and became part of the entourage of the new emperor and his son Titus, to whom completion of the capture of Jerusalem was entrusted. Hence Josephus witnessed from the vantage of the Roman headquarters both the siege of Jerusalem from March 70 CE and the destruction of the city in August of that year. According to the *Jewish War*, he made numerous attempts to persuade his former comrades to surrender and throw themselves on the mercy of Titus (5.362–419; 6.94–113, 365), but in vain.

Josephus was granted by Titus the special privilege of rescuing some of his friends from crucifixion during the mass executions that followed the fall of Jerusalem, although in some cases it was too late to prevent them from dying from their wounds. He was also permitted to save a large number of books from destruction. But soon he was far away from the dismal sight of his destroyed homeland and ensconced in Rome, granted a place to live in the house where Vespasian had lived before he had become emperor. With a guaranteed income from land granted to him out of imperial munificence and granted Roman citizenship, Josephus could have retired into a pampered life of leisure on the fringes of the court.[3]

So far as is known, Josephus remained in Rome for the rest of his life, but it is much to the benefit of later generations that instead of leisure he chose to write books. The *Jewish War* was composed in the main within a decade of the end of the war itself. It was prompted, according to Josephus's introductory remarks (1.1–2), by a desire to set the record straight in response to various unnamed accounts which did not do proper justice to the importance of the conflict (and, by implication, its primary protagonists, who included not only Vespasian and Titus but also Josephus himself). The *Jewish War* was followed in the eighties and early nineties by a mammoth undertaking to compose, in twenty books of *Jewish Antiquities*, a continuous narrative covering the whole history of the Jews from Creation down to the outbreak of the war against Rome in 66 CE. Josephus's decision to add to the *Antiquities* when they were published in 93 CE a brief autobiographical account (his *Life*), focusing on his career as a rebel commander in Galilee in 66–67 CE, suggests that his position in Rome was less secure than he wished and that enemies had thrown doubt on the genuineness of his enthusiasm for Roman rule over his homeland.

It is worth noting, in light of the doubts cast by later generations on his loyalty to his Jewish identity, that he did not see any reason to defend himself in the *Life* on that score. Indeed, in his final surviving work, the two books known as *Against Apion*, which were probably written in the mid-nineties, he presented a robust defense of the Jewish claim to antiquity and an apologia for the Jewish constitution established by Moses, for which he invented a new term, 'theocracy,' to explain its superiority to all preceding forms of government.[4]

In *Against Apion*, as in all his writings, Josephus defined himself very clearly as a Jew, and in describing the customs of the Jews he made frequent use of the first–person plural. Through the account of his role during the revolt in the *Jewish War* and the revelations in his *Life*, his career is far better known than that of any other historian from the early Roman Empire, even if, as with any autobiography, the author's self-representation must be treated with some skepticism. The autobiography of the orator Nicolaus of Damascus, who had once been court historian to Herod the Great and ended his days in Rome in the time of Augustus, provided one model for Josephus as an intellectual. But in the Roman world in which Josephus was living by the nineties, the publication of a self-serving account of political events in which the author had been a major actor was a well-established tradition—in the late Republic Sulla had written twenty-two books of memoirs, and Cicero had written about his achievements both in Latin and in Greek—and Josephus's *Life* was similarly intended as a political apologia. His attempts to gloss over his complex relationship during the Galilean campaign with other Jewish leaders—including on the one hand his bête noir John of Gischala, who in 68 emerged in Jerusalem as one of the leaders of resistance to Rome, and on the other hand the Herodian king Agrippa II who fought on the side of the Romans—need to be read alongside his vainglorious narrative in the *Jewish War* of his activities in the same campaign. The two accounts do not match. The discrepancies have occasionally been attributed to faulty memory, the use of different sources, or simple sloppiness, but Josephus's attempt to set the record straight later in life has provided, rather ironically, much of the ammunition for those who have been inclined to doubt his reliability altogether.[5]

Such doubts are reasonable, but it is less justifiable to put into question Josephus's dedication to his Jewish heritage. Rome in the last decades of the first century CE was not a good place to be a Jew. The imperial dynasty founded by Vespasian and Titus based its legitimacy on propaganda about the great victory over the Jews. The destruction of Jerusalem was celebrated by the regime long after the fall of the city: as late as 86 CE, coins of Titus's younger brother Domitian still harked back to 'Judaea capta' with an image of a weeping captive Jewess bound under a palm tree. The Arch of Titus, erected just a few years earlier, portrayed the procession in which the *menorah* and other precious objects from Jerusalem had been carried in triumph through the streets of Rome in 71. Jews were not allowed to rebuild the Temple of their God; instead, they were required to pay an annual tax to Jupiter Capitolinus in Rome.[6]

Flavius Josephus—as a new Roman citizen, Josephus was accorded the name of his benefactor, Titus Flavius Vespasianus—could have adopted a purely Roman persona, as had the former Roman governor of Judaea, Tiberius Julius Alexander, who had been born a Jew but abandoned the religion of his ancestors. But Josephus chose instead to emphasize in the *Jewish War* his status as a Jew, describing himself as 'a Hebrew by race, a native of Jerusalem, and a priest' (1.3), and in his later works he wrote, with passion and at great length, about his Jewish heritage. So far as is known, he had no need to write anything at all, and, if he was going to write, he could have chosen a neutral subject that would not draw attention to the striking divergence between the denigration of Judaism by the regime and his own advocacy of his ancestral tradition.

It is therefore rather bizarre that Josephus has so often been judged as a cowardly traitor to his people on the basis of his surrender to the Romans during the war and his flattery of Vespasian and Titus in his account of their conduct of the Judaean campaign. There were undoubtedly constraints on what an author could publish in elite circles in imperial Rome without risking the ire of the regime, and anything that Josephus wrote was inevitably enthusiastic about his patrons to a degree that may feel uncomfortable to modern readers. But it cannot be denied that his decision to write so copiously and positively about the Jewish tradition was itself an act of exceptional bravery in a world where it was often safer to say nothing at all.

The Book

The book was actually composed in the form of seven books. Although his ostensible subject was the war between the Jews and the Romans over just four years (66–70 CE), Josephus chose to begin his narrative more than two centuries earlier, with the revolt of the Maccabees against the Seleucid king Antiochus IV in the 160s BCE engendered by Antiochus's attempt to turn the Jerusalem Temple into a place for worship of a pagan god. By the end of book 1 the reader is still learning about the rule of Herod in Judaea in the late first century BCE, and the narrative reaches the outbreak of the revolt only in the middle of book 2. The quite detailed narrative of the end of Herod's reign and his death in 4 BCE, for which Josephus could use a contemporary account by Nicolaus of Damascus, was followed by a very skimpy treatment of the rule of Herod's son Archelaus as ethnarch of Judaea from 4 BCE to 6 CE and the first three decades of direct rule of Judaea by Roman governors. Josephus may well have been hampered by a lack of surviving evidence for the events of those years. If dry accounts by Roman governors such as Pontius Pilate had been sent to Rome and shelved somewhere in the city, it seems that Josephus did not use them. The gap is papered over by an extended description of the Essenes, a group of pious ascetics whose distinctive lifestyle is presented as admirable. Josephus's ostensible reason for what might otherwise seem an irrelevant excursus is to describe the Essenes, along with the Pharisees and Sadducees, as the respectable philosophies of Judaism in order to compare them to the anarchic doctrines of a certain Judas of Galilee. Judas's assertion that Jews should obey no master other than God was held responsible not only for widespread unrest in 6 CE, when a census was imposed at the start of Roman rule, but also for the final cataclysm that led to the loss of the Temple over sixty years later.

The vicissitudes of the Temple provide the framework of the history as a whole, from its salvation by the Maccabees to its destruction in August 70 in a fire described in detail with expressionist anguish in book 6. The narrative, which had covered a century and a half in book 1, slows down as it begins to cover the war itself. Events in the year 66 CE are described in detail in the second half of book 2. The following year, which included Josephus's campaign in Galilee, is allotted the remainder of book 2 and all of book 3. The years 68 and 69, which were less eventful in Judaea because Vespasian ceased campaigning following news of the death of the emperor Nero, were covered in book 4. But from the start of book 5, which narrates the beginning of the assault on Jerusalem in spring of 70 CE, the story is followed first month by month, then week by week, and eventually (in book 6) day by day as the city burns, with readers invited to linger on descriptions of particular horror, such as a story about a certain Mary who was reduced by famine to roasting and eating her baby (6.199–218).

Focus on such abominations allows Josephus to ruminate on the causes of the disaster, emphasizing divine punishment for the sins of the rebel leaders among the Jews and the wickedness of their fratricidal struggles, which continued within the city until the last stages of the siege. The power of the divine over human affairs is a theme that surfaces frequently in the history, and Josephus is at pains to point out that God sends clear warnings to those prepared to take heed: the prophecies of a certain Jesus son of Ananias about the imminent destruction had been mocked in 63 CE but proved seven years later to have been all too accurate (6.300–309). Among those to whom divine revelation had been specially vouchsafed was Josephus himself—hence his prophecy at Jotapata. When Josephus portrayed himself as an actor in the history, he called himself 'Josephus', using the third person, reserving the first–person singular for observations in his authorial voice. It was as a participant in the action that he was portrayed as a latter-day Jeremiah, urging the defenders of Jerusalem to surrender on the basis that this was the will of God (5.391–92).

In narrative terms the end of book 6, with its summary of the history of Jerusalem over the centuries before the destruction just described, provided a satisfactory culmination. Book 7, which deals with the aftermath of the war, is something of an anticlimax, notwithstanding the set piece descriptions of the triumphal procession of Vespasian and Titus in Rome in 71 CE and of the dramatic fall of Masada in 74 CE and the heroic death by their own hands of the Jewish defenders of the fortress. It is possible that book 7, in which Titus's younger brother Domitian plays a more prominent role than in the first six books, was added to the history by Josephus when Domitian became emperor in 81 CE after Titus's death. If this was the case, Josephus must have adapted at the same time the introduction to book 1 in which the contents of the seventh book are described

(1.29–30). The promulgation of different versions of a literary work was not unusual in the ancient world, where publication took place essentially through public readings. Harder to evaluate is the relationship of the *Jewish War* as it survives in Greek and the version that Josephus claimed to have written earlier in his native language (presumably Aramaic) and circulated to the non–Greek speakers in the interior (1.3), so that 'Parthians, Babylonians, deepest Arabia, and my compatriots in Mesopotamia and Adiabene had accurate information about the origin of the war, its painful progress, and its conclusion' (1.6). The book as it survives is replete with the characteristics of Greek historiography, as we shall see, and it is unlikely that the Aramaic version (if it indeed really existed) bore any resemblance to it.

According to Josephus himself, the Greek version of the *Jewish War* was composed in order to inform Greeks and those Romans not involved in the campaign about what had happened. This would not preclude a Jewish readership, of course, but the title of the book was Josephus's (as can be seen from his references to it in his later writings) and presupposed a non-Jewish perspective—from the Jewish point of view, the story concerned a Roman rather than a Jewish war. Josephus was in fact explicit that he wished to counter earlier accounts of the campaigns that, by disparaging the strength of the Jewish forces which had been suppressed (1.7–8), failed to give the Roman generals due credit. Writers of contemporary history under intolerant emperors could inevitably be accused after the event of pandering to the interests of the regime on which they depended, and in a subsequent generation Tacitus wrote with scorn and horror about the curbs on freedom of speech under the Flavian dynasty, and especially Domitian. It was certainly the case that some works of contemporary history under the patronage of emperors, such as the history of Rome completed by Velleius Paterculus in, or just before, 31 CE, were little more than vehicles for imperial propaganda. But it did not have to be so. Orators wrote knowingly about the possibilities of figured speech through which subversive messages could be inscribed within a literary text without the risk of censorship through too blunt a message.

Certainly much in the *Jewish War* ran counter to the messages widely promulgated by Vespasian and Titus to the Roman people. Josephus might be scrupulously polite about the heroism and wisdom of his imperial patrons, but his insistence that they had won their glorious victory only through the aid of the God of the Jews did not accord well with the self-representation of a regime that gloried in the destruction of the Temple of that God. Nor did Josephus's repeated claim that this destruction had been the undesired result of indiscipline within the Roman ranks rather than the culmination of an efficient military strategy.

In some ways, therefore, the *Jewish War* can be regarded as a work of Roman literature. But it was also the product of a learned Jewish education, and in many respects its form owes most to the conventions of Greek historiography as they had developed since the fifth century BCE. Many motifs in the book, such as the appeals to biblical precedents in the speech Josephus put into his own mouth when addressing the rebels from outside the walls of Jerusalem (5.375–419), would have made sense only to Jewish readers. Jews had been writing extensively in Greek for some four hundred years, inspired not least by the Septuagint version of the biblical text, which was the work of translators of the third and second centuries BCE. Some Jews, like Philo of Alexandria in the first half of the first century CE, expressed their Judaism in the guise of Greek philosophy. Other Jews explained their religious heritage in Greek poetry and even, in the case of the *Exagoge* of Ezekiel the Tragedian, in the form of drama. At least one Jew besides Josephus wrote a history of the war of 66 to 70, since its author, Justus of Tiberias, was accused by Josephus of having lied.[7]

Most such Jewish historiography composed in Greek is known now only through fragmentary citations by Christians in later centuries, and it is unclear to what extent Josephus felt himself to be writing within an established Jewish literary genre. More certain is his blatant debt to specific trends within Greek historiography as a whole. The opening of book 1, with its grandiose assertion that 'the war fought by the Jews against the Romans was not only the greatest war of our time but could well be one of the greatest collisions between states or nations of which word has come down to us' (1.1), will have instantly reminded ancient readers of the opening of Thucydides's *Peloponnesian War*, which claimed that the war between Sparta and Athens in the fifth century BCE was the greatest war of all time. By evoking Thucydides, who had sought to explain history by searching for the causes of events, Josephus prepared his readers for a similarly sober analysis. They will have been reminded also of the use of Thucydides's scientific approach in the second century BCE by Polybius, a Greek intellectual who, like Josephus, had written about the Roman conquest of his homeland while living in exile among the Roman elite. Josephus, like Polybius, brought to the capital a provincial's perspective on the violent conquests on the fringes of the empire that enabled the pampered luxury of the imperial city.[8]

Josephus stated in *Against Apion* (1.50) that, as a non-native speaker, he had required assistance with his Greek in writing the *Jewish War*, but the book is replete with rhetorical techniques of considerable sophistication. It was a feature of Greek historiography since the fifth century BCE that speeches were composed by the author to put into the mouths of characters. These speeches were designed to explain what should have been said as much as what was actually said at the time, and the speeches in the *Jewish War* are carefully crafted. Less obvious for a writer in the Thucydidean tradition was Josephus's frequent appeal to pathos, and he explicitly apologized to his readers for allowing his emotions at the destruction of Jerusalem to spill over into the text (1.11–12). The apology conceals much artifice, since he was capable, when he desired, of shifting focus fully from the Jewish viewpoint to the Roman and back—it is disconcerting, for instance, that his description of the Roman triumph in book 7 is a wholly positive account seen from the Roman side despite the sacrilege to the Temple treasures carried in the procession. At times his descriptions are almost filmic, as when he encourages his readers to imagine the groans emitted by the Jews as flames shot forth from the Temple and the fire took hold (6.272–76).

The *Jewish War* is not prefaced by any dedication, unlike Josephus's later works, which are presented as commissioned by a patron named Epaphroditus (who has proved impossible to identify with any certainty). There is no reason to believe that the book was commissioned by the regime—indeed, in view of the frequent dissonance between imperial propaganda and Josephus's message, such a commission is highly unlikely. But Josephus himself in 93 CE claimed in the *Life* (361) that he had presented the books to the emperors themselves 'when the events had hardly passed out of sight,' and that Titus had been so anxious that the *Jewish War* should be treated as the sole authority for this history that he affixed his own signature to the books and gave orders for their publication, while Agrippa II had written no fewer than sixty-two letters to testify to the truth of the record (363–64).

A few years later, in *Against Apion* (50–52), Josephus stated that he had presented his volumes not only to the emperors but also to many other Romans who had taken part in the campaigns. He contrasted these free presentation copies for Romans to those he sold to many of 'ours' (that is, Jews) who were well versed in Greek learning. Of these, he named in particular three members of the Herodian dynasty, culminating in the 'most remarkable' King Agrippa himself. Josephus claimed that all these readers bore testimony to the truth of his account. One can well imagine that they checked carefully that their own participation in the traumatic events Josephus described had been portrayed in an appropriately positive manner.

The *Jewish War* was a fine work of almost instant history, composed in the immediate aftermath of a dramatic campaign of great political significance not just for the Jews but for the whole Roman world. The book must have relied on a variety of sources, including the universal history composed by Herod's court historian, Nicolaus of Damascus, and Vespasian's memoir of the conduct of the Judaean campaign, to which Josephus referred in his autobiography (*Life* 342,

358), but Josephus was an author rather than a compiler and placed his own stamp on the narrative. Nonetheless, the *Jewish War* was not a great work of literature. No one was likely to read the book in order to enjoy and profit from Josephus's Greek style, and it is unlikely that any ordinary Greek or Roman would have dipped into the text for aesthetic pleasure.

It is quite likely that a copy of the *Jewish War* was kept in the library of the Temple of Peace, erected near the forum in Rome by Vespasian as a memorial to the pacification of the Jews and endowed with commemorative art objects from the Jerusalem Temple (7.158–62), but that does not mean the book was read. In the early second century Suetonius mentioned the name of Josephus as the prophet who had predicted correctly that Vespasian would become emperor, but he did not record that Josephus had written a history of the war. There is no trace of the *Jewish War* in the surviving sections of the long account of the events leading up to the siege of Jerusalem in the *Histories* written by Suetonius's contemporary Tacitus, even though he, like Suetonius, may well have come across Josephus in Rome in the last decades of the first century and certainly could have read his writings. Cassius Dio, who wrote his *Roman History* in the early third century, more than a hundred years after Tacitus, also seems to have ignored the *Jewish War* when he recounted the Judaean campaign, notwithstanding his knowledge of a Jew named Josephus who had predicted after his capture by Vespasian that Vespasian would release him within a year on becoming emperor. According to the Christian author Eusebius, writing in the fourth century, Josephus was honored in Rome by the erection of a statue. If the story is true, the statue may have commemorated his role as prophet more than his reputation as an author.[9]

If by the third century (at the latest) most ordinary Greeks and Romans had lost interest in Josephus's *Jewish War*, who continued to read the book, and why?

Early Years (100–1450)

CHAPTER 2

The Book among Early Christians (100–600)

The survival of the *Jewish War* after its first generation of readers can be credited entirely to the early Church and especially to the interest of Christians in the fulfillment of Jesus's prophecies, as reported in the Gospels, of the forthcoming destruction of Jerusalem and its famous Temple. For the rest of antiquity, the book had a life only within the Church.

The first Christians were Jews, but already in the decades immediately following the crucifixion of Jesus the Christian message was spread to gentiles in cities around the eastern Mediterranean. By the outbreak of war in Jerusalem in 66 CE many of these Christians had begun to define themselves as a new religious community defined by their faith in salvation through Christ. But a full parting of the ways between Judaism and Christianity occurred only gradually, and at different times in different places, over the course of the first four centuries CE. Throughout this process one impetus to the parting was the need of Christians to define the relationship of their new faith to what they viewed as the old covenant of God with the Jews. And one puzzling aspect of that covenant was the willingness of the Almighty to allow his Temple to be destroyed in 70 CE. Josephus's detailed narrative, which explained the disaster so clearly in theological terms as a punishment of the Jews for their sins, provided a perfect explanation.[1]

By the end of antiquity the *Jewish War* thus became one of the books most commonly cited by Christian authors. But this status was not acquired immediately. In the second and third centuries of the Church, the *Jewish War* was not read as much as other works of Josephus: Christians like Clement, Tertullian, Irenaeus, and Origen turned more to the *Antiquities* to clarify the text of the Old Testament, and to *Against Apion* to serve as a model for the burgeoning genre of Christian apologetic. But the *Jewish War* was at least known to Christians by the mid-second century, when Theophilus of Antioch referred to Josephus as the author of a history of 'the Jewish war which they waged with the Romans', and a few years later Minucius Felix bracketed Josephus's history with the account of the Roman historian Marcus Antonius Julianus, who had been procurator of Judaea from 66 to 70 CE, asserting that Josephus's work could be read as testimony that the sufferings of the Jews came upon them as punishment for their abandonment of God.[2] And striking similarities between the set-piece description provided by Josephus in the *Jewish War* (2.116–61) and an account of the Jewish philosophies (including a long description of the monastic lifestyle and distinctive beliefs of the ascetic Essenes) in the *Philosophoumena* of the Christian author Hippolytus, who is generally thought to have written in the third century, probably reflect Christian borrowing from Josephus's book, even if the words of Josephus reached Hippolytus only indirectly.[3]

Explicit citations of the *Jewish War* begin to be found slightly later in the third century in the works of the indefatigable scholar Origen of Caesarea and, in the early fourth century, in the writings of the Church historian Eusebius. But although the impact of Eusebius on the reverent treatment of Josephus by later Christians would be immense, this was less because of his use of the *Jewish War* than because he was the first Christian known to have quoted verbatim the so-called *Testimonium Flavianum*, a brief passage about the life and career of Jesus which can be found in nearly all manuscripts of book 18 of Josephus's *Antiquities*. It was probably on the basis of the *Testimonium* that the reputation of Josephus as a source of incalculable value for Christians was so secure that Jerome, at the end of the fourth century, included him in his Christian history of literature, *On Illustrious Men*. Jerome's contemporary, Basil of Caesarea, asserted that Josephus had written his Jewish history 'for us' (i.e., for Christians). The significance of Josephus's testimony for these authors consisted in his status as an independent witness to Christian traditions, either as a 'Jew' (meaning a predecessor of contemporary Jews) or as a 'Hebrew' (meaning a predecessor to Christianity).[4]

Eusebius's *Ecclesiastical History* employed extended citations of the *Jewish War* in aid of an interpretation of Jewish history that blamed the fall of Jerusalem on the Jewish plot against Christ. Hence Eusebius's citation of Josephus's description of the multitude of Jews who had flowed into Jerusalem for the Passover in 70 CE and as a result were 'shut up inside Jerusalem as if in a prison': 'Indeed, it was because in those same days in which they had inflicted all the sufferings of the passion on the Saviour and Benefactor of all, Christ the Lord, they must needs be reassembled as if in a prison to be meted out the death intended for them by divine justice.' The same claim was found earlier in Origen, who took Josephus to task for not having realized the causal connection, but it was greatly expanded by Eusebius, who related both the portents described by Josephus and Josephus's graphic tale of the woman Mary who had been reduced to eating her baby (6.199–219) as evidence of divine punishment.

Eusebius's enterprise of writing the history of the Church as an institution was in itself an innovation that was to have a remarkable impact on Christian self-understanding in ensuing generations, and his endorsement of the value of the *Jewish War* thus brought the book into the center of Christian life. The argument of the ecclesiastical history, which traced the story of the salvation of mankind through Christ and the Church, encouraged the practice of copying the *Jewish War* in the manuscripts of Josephus's works not in chronological order of composition but after the *Antiquities*, to provide the culmination of the Jewish story that had begun with the Creation. Indeed, in many manuscripts the name of the book was changed from Josephus's own title to *Halosis*, 'Conquest', to reflect the Christian notion that the destruction of Jerusalem was the moral of the story.[5]

The requirements of Christian rhetoric which stimulated Eusebius's employment of the *Jewish War* in his ecclesiastical history sometimes encouraged reticence about his reliance on the book elsewhere. So, for instance, when he cited the pagan philosopher Porphyry in his *Preparation for the Gospel* as testimony to the excellence of the Essenes, he seems to have deemed it prudent to avoid mentioning that Porphyry had stated openly his own reliance on Josephus: it was more helpful for Eusebius's argument to portray the

Greek sage as an independent admirer of these ascetic predecessors of Christianity. Josephus's value as an external authority, used to bolster the Christian tradition precisely because he was outside Christianity, needed to be balanced against an increasing tendency to treat him, as Cassiodorus termed him in the sixth century, as 'one of our fathers'.[6]

By the fifth century the *Jewish War* had become the most important of Josephus's writings for Christian authors when they engaged in anti-Jewish polemic. In Antioch in Syria, John Chrysostom cited Josephus's history as a tragic narrative, and Cyril of Alexandria treated Josephus's whole story simply as an account of the punishment of the Jews for the murder of Christ. A favorite passage was Mary's eating of her baby in book 6, which was taken as the fulfillment of biblical prophecy.

The cannibalism story had been cited already in the second century in the anti-Jewish tractate on the Passover by Melito of Sardis, but without any indication that it came from Josephus. In Melito's work the story may indeed have been no more than a reflection of Lamentations 4:10. But as the *Jewish War* became almost a canonical Christian text, to be read alongside the New Testament as an account of the consequences for the Jews rejecting Christ, it was increasing important that Josephus be treated as historically trustworthy. For Jerome in the early fifth century, Josephus was the 'Greek Livy', a judgment echoed in the middle of the sixth century by Cassiodorus, who referred to him as 'almost a second Livy'.[7]

Cassiodorus played a pivotal role in the preservation of many classical writings through the intensive copying and translating of manuscripts in his monastery in Italy. He was responsible for commissioning Latin translations by his

FIGURE 2.1 Titus and Josephus, and Mary eating her baby. Miniature in a manuscript of a Latin translation of the *Jewish War*. Bibliothèque Nationale, Paris (Latin 16730, fol. 262v).

friends in ca. 576 CE of Josephus's *Antiquities* and *Against Apion*, 'a task involving great labour on their part since he [Josephus] is subtle and complex.' But he wrote that a Latin version of what he called the '*Jewish Captivity*' was already available in a version that, according to Cassiodorus, was variously ascribed to Jerome, Ambrose, or Rufinus, and that therefore no new translation was required. Cassiodorus noted that 'the fact that this translation is ascribed to such men, declares the special merits of its composition.' It is improbable in light of such praise that the Latin version to which Cassiodorus referred was the very literal translation found in manuscripts from the ninth century (see below). It is more likely that he had in mind a Latin paraphrase of the *Jewish War* that had been widely available since the last quarter of the fourth century CE. This paraphrase was almost certainly composed by none of these great theologians, and it is an irony, in view of its huge influence, that so little is known about the process by which the *Jewish War* made its way through this paraphrase into the Latin-speaking world.[8]

This Latin paraphrase is usually attributed to Josephus in manuscripts written before the ninth century, but it is generally attributed in the later medieval manuscripts, of which many survive, to Egesippus or Hegesippus. The name 'Hegesippus' seems to have been a corruption of the Latin 'Iosippus', but it was popularized by a confusion with a Christian writer of the second century CE whose *Hypomnemata* ('Memoranda') were used by Eusebius and Jerome as a source for the history of the Church. The author of the Latin Josephus paraphrase is thus commonly named 'Ps.-Hegesippus' to distinguish him from his older namesake, with whom he had nothing else in common either in purpose or in outlook. The translation had presumably been promulgated anonymously, since (despite Cassiodorus) Jerome stated explicitly that he did not translate Josephus. No ancient list of the works of Ambrose or Rufinus mentions a translation of the *Jewish War*, although the belief that Ambrose had been the translator of the paraphrase lingered on well into the Middle Ages.

Ps.-Hegesippus's paraphrase is usually referred to by ancient writers as *De excidio urbis Hierosolymitanae* ('On the Destruction of the City of Jerusalem'). The author followed the outlines of Josephus's narrative, but in five books rather than seven, and with a stress on divine retribution, Christian triumphalism, and the most sensational aspects of the siege as found in the original. The demise of the Jewish polity is described with some relish, with a drastically simplified and shortened version of Josephus's account of the complex relations between the warring Jewish factions. In fact the author made no attempt to disguise the fact that he was not simply translating Josephus's text. Thus he cited Josephus a number of times as though he was an author different from the source of his main narrative. And he occasionally introduced new material not to be found in the *Jewish War*, such as a long passage about Simon Magus, as well as the distinctively Christian theology that permeates the work. Nonetheless, Ps.-Hegesippus's paraphrase was often ascribed directly to Josephus in the Middle Ages, so that it was included in some manuscripts of the works of Josephus and attributed to Josephus in some medieval book lists. Hence confusion between the 'real' Josephus and this Christianized version was common in the Latin West in the later medieval period.[9]

By the end of the first millennium knowledge of the *Jewish War* from Ps.-Hegesippus was supplemented for Latin readers from two other sources. One was the translation into Latin by Rufinus already in the early fifth century CE of the excerpts of the *Jewish War* found in Eusebius's *Ecclesiastical History*. Rufinus's version of these excerpts is much closer to the original Greek than Ps.-Hegesippus's paraphrase, but it is often rhetorical and dramatic. It contrasts markedly with a very literal Latin rendering of the whole text of the *Jewish War* found in manuscripts from the ninth century. This literal translation was to be frequently copied and much read by Christians in the West throughout the Middle Ages and well into the early modern period. We do not know who produced this translation or when (although evidently it existed by the time it was copied in the ninth century). The ascription in some fifteenth-century manuscripts to Rufinus was clearly an error based on a misunderstanding of Cassiodorus, but reference to the translator as '[Rufinus]' is sometimes used by writers nowadays as a way to differentiate this version from Ps.-Hegesippus's paraphrase.[10]

By the end of antiquity the stage was thus set in both Greek and Latin Christendom for Christian readings of the *Jewish War*. Josephus, who had expended so much energy to demonstrate that disaster had come to the Jews as a result of the sins of tyrants and their followers in the faction fighting he described within Jerusalem, would have been astonished and horrified at the reinterpretation of his narrative as a divine judgment on his people for rejection of Christ. He might have hoped, at the very least, for a more sympathetic reading of his history by fellow Jews, but, as we shall see, it would take many centuries, after the flurry of interest in his lifetime, before Jews paid any attention at all to his book.

The Book among Jews (100–1450)

It may seem sad, in light of Josephus's brave efforts in his final decades in Rome to write in defense of his people, that it is impossible to demonstrate that any Jew knew about him or to his writings for over eight centuries after his death, but this striking silence actually reveals more about the vagaries of the survival of Jewish literature from antiquity than it does about the Jewish reception of Josephus and his book.

We know, of course, from Josephus's later writings that the *Jewish War* had a Jewish readership while he was alive, and, indeed, that some of the responses of his compatriots to what he had written elicited the clarifications about his career as a general in Galilee to be found in his autobiography. His later writings sometimes presuppose in part a non-Roman readership, as when he explains Roman customs in the *Antiquities*, and it is reasonable to assume that some of these will have been Greek-speaking Jews. Greek remained the language of the Jewish communities in the city of Rome at least to the fifth century CE, as can be seen from the grave monuments found in the catacombs. Greek was the language of liturgy for Jews elsewhere in the Mediterranean diaspora still in the sixth century CE, when the Byzantine emperor Justinian attempted to impose regulations on the Greek translations of the Bible to be used in synagogues. We can therefore assume a potential Jewish readership for the Greek text of the *Jewish War* down to the end of late antiquity. For Jews, the catastrophic story of the destruction of Jerusalem and the Temple lost none of its urgency over the passing years. On the contrary, the refusal of the Roman state to permit the restoration of the sacrificial worship mandated in the Torah was a continuing affront. Why, then, is it so hard to find any clear trace that any ancient Jews read the *Jewish War* after the beginning of the second century CE?[11]

The events of 66 to 70 loom large in extant Jewish literature from the second to the sixth centuries, but they seem to come from a historical tradition in Hebrew and Aramaic preserved in parallel with Josephus's *Jewish War* rather than from the *Jewish War* itself. Most striking is the emergence over centuries within rabbinic sources of a legend about Rabban Yohanan ben Zakkai, a rabbinic sage who lived through the war and its aftermath. This legend has close similarities to some aspects of the account of Josephus's surrender to Vespasian at Jotapata in the *Jewish War*. In documents from the earliest stratum of the rabbinic corpus such as the Mishnah, which was compiled in the early third century CE, Yohanan features only as a leader within a small study circle at Yavneh, a small town in the Mediterranean coastal plain of Judaea. His main activities are discussing developments in Jewish law, including changes to liturgy required to adapt to the end of the Temple cult, such as new rules for when and where the *shofar* should be blown on New Year and the *lulav* and *ethrog* waved on the festival of Tabernacles. But some three centuries later various versions of a story about his relations with the Roman authorities during and after the war feature in rabbinic texts. According to this story, Yohanan had worked before the revolt to avoid conflict with Rome, outwitted the extremists among the rebels in order to escape the city by a ruse when it was under siege, prophesied to Vespasian that he would become emperor, and requested successfully from the emperor the right to set up his academy in Yavneh after the war. The parallels to Josephus's self-description in the *Jewish War* are obvious—as are the differences.[12]

The fact that the Yohanan legend emerged in the fifth century may reflect only the way that genres of rabbinic literature expanded more into storytelling in this period compared to the compendia of legal rulings and Bible interpretation characteristic of earlier rabbinic generations. But it may also reflect a shift toward greater interest in history in general—and especially in the history of the late Second Temple period, when the fall of Jerusalem could be attributed, according to the Babylonian Talmud, to 'causeless hatred'. It is reasonable to surmise that some stories about the last days of the Temple came to the rabbis in Babylonia in the fourth century CE, at the same time as Christianity reached Mesopotamia from the eastern Roman provinces. Some of the traditions now found in *Lamentations Rabbah* may have been adopted by rabbis in Palestine in the same period to combat Christian historiography. But, although in principle Babylonian rabbis could have learned from the Aramaic first draft of the *Jewish War* composed for their ancestors before the Greek version was written, it is highly unlikely that they did. The great set pieces of the *Jewish War*, from Jotapata to Gamala to Titus's council of war in 70 CE to Masada, are absent from rabbinic consciousness up to and including the composition of the Babylonian Talmud around 600 CE. The rabbis did not read Josephus.[13]

Back in the first century the rabbis had constituted only one of many varieties of Judaism, and the impression that their literary choices were shared by all Jews may well be mistaken. The contrary is hard to prove primarily because the rabbis produced a literature in Hebrew and Aramaic and seem similarly to have restricted their reading to Semitic languages. There was nothing inevitable about such self-restriction, since Greek was widely spoken in Roman Palestine at the time of the Mishnah and the Palestinian

Talmud, and Christians not far from the neighborhood of the rabbis who produced the Babylonian Talmud knew enough Greek to engage in intensive translations of Greek theological works into Syriac, a Semitic language closely akin to Babylonian Jewish Aramaic. Ignoring Greek Jewish literature was thus a cultural choice by the rabbis, who constituted a self-perpetuating scholastic movement within Judaism characterized by devotion to the transmission of traditional interpretations of the Torah by word of mouth. The focus of rabbinic teaching was on the best way to be an adult male Jew. Rabbinic interest in the outside world was thus largely confined to its impact on Jewish religious life. The Temple's destruction was lamented. Rome was generally portrayed as the wicked kingdom, equated with Edom, the ancestral enemy of Israel, and traditions about Vespasian and Titus focused on exotic speculation about the sufferings of Titus in the afterlife as punishment for his sins. The geographic horizons of the rabbis were essentially limited to the two centers of their activity in Palestine and Babylonia, and it is not certain how much influence rabbis exerted on the Mediterranean diaspora before the rise of Islam.

It is therefore less surprising than it might have seemed at first sight that the rabbis should have ignored the *Jewish War*, since they also ignored all the rest of Jewish literature in Greek. The extensive output of the philosopher Philo, an older contemporary of Josephus, survives only because it was adopted and copied by Christians. The same is true of the apocrypha, those Jewish writings in Greek considered scriptural by Jews who read the Septuagint as their Bible, and therefore also by early Christians who incorporated them into their Old Testament, but absent from the Hebrew Bible of the rabbis. A few stories from the Greek biblical tradition, such as the martyrdom of Hannah and her children, which is found in its fullest form in the Greek book of 2 Maccabees, found their way in garbled form into the rabbinic tradition, but most were simply unknown to rabbinic Jews, in much the same way as the *Jewish War*.

Until, that is, the tenth century, when the *Jewish War* made its entry into the canon of rabbinic literature in altered form and by a roundabout way. The Hebrew book known as *Sefer Yosippon*, which narrated the history of the Jewish people down to the destruction of the Second Temple in 70 CE, was compiled from a paraphrase of a number of works in Latin, including Jerome's Latin Old Testament (the Vulgate), parts of Vergil's *Aeneid*, Livy's Roman history, Orosius's *History against the Pagans*, and the (Cassiodoran) Latin translation of Josephus's *Jewish Antiquities*. But chapters 51 to 89 turned to the *Jewish War* through an adapted version of Ps.-Hegesippus's *On the Destruction of the City of Jerusalem*. It followed the literary structure of Ps.-Hegesippus's work and shared with Ps.-Hegesippus the omission of such major episodes in the *Jewish War* as Josephus's claim at Jotapata to be a prophet and the account of the deliberations about suicide by the Sicarii on Masada, which was such an important feature in book 7 of Josephus's original work.[14]

The author and purpose of *Sefer Yosippon* are unknown, as are the date and place of its composition. But it is striking that the sources used were all in Latin rather than Greek, and it is therefore plausible to place the author in Italy after the demise of Greek as the language of Italian Jews (at least in their epigraphy) in the middle of the first millennium CE. More precise dating is impossible, not least because the text was quite frequently redacted into different forms through the Middle Ages. The colophon of one manuscript dates to 953 CE and shows that a version of *Sefer Yosippon* was extant by then, but an earlier version may be reflected in fragments of the text found in the Cairo Genizah. In view of the frequent rewriting of the text, the reference in chapter 1 of *Sefer Yosippon* to Hungarians living by the Danube, which could have been written only after 895 CE, does not provide a date for the first version of the book as a whole. On the other hand, one striking deviation by the author from the Ps.-Hegesippus text from which he worked would support the hypothesis that the first version of *Sefer Yosippon* was produced in southern Italy not long before the book was copied in 953. Where Ps.-Hegesippus had followed the *Jewish War* in describing the mass suicide of the defenders of Masada at the hands of each other, the author of *Sefer Yosippon* stated that only the women and children were killed and that the men fought to the death against the Romans. The change is unlikely to be accidental. It probably reflects debates within Judaism about the ideal of martyrdom to be found in earlier rabbinic stories about R. Akiva's heroic suffering at the hands of the Romans. Such debates may have been sparked in reaction to notions of martyrdom as an aspect of holy war to be found among both Muslims and Christians in the Saracen invasions of Italy in this period.[15]

The suicides at Masada were not the only changes made by the author of *Sefer Yosippon* to Ps.-Hegesippus's paraphrase of the *Jewish War*, since he clearly found it necessary to expunge the Christian explanations for the Jews' sufferings that permeated his source. Passages in Ps.-Hegesippus that blamed the Jews for the murder of Jesus were omitted and the cause of the destruction was found instead in the faction fighting among the Jews and the sacrilegious spilling of blood in the Temple, as in Josephus's original version.

These alterations seem to have been the independent work of the author of the *Sefer Yosippon*—he does not seem to have known anything about Josephus's book in Greek or about the literal translation into Latin that in later centuries was ascribed to Rufinus. It is unknown why his Hebrew history was from an early stage attributed not to Joseph the son of Matthias, the general who, according to the *Jewish War* (2.568), commanded the rebel forces in Galilee at the start of the war (that is, the historian Josephus), but to Joseph the son of Gorion, who, according to the *Jewish War* (2.563), was elected at the same time to serve as commander in chief alongside the former high priest Ananus son of Ananus. The attribution cannot have arisen from anything Josephus wrote about Joseph the son of Gorion because, in contrast to extensive discussion of the career and fate of Ananus, nothing more is heard about Joseph the son of Gorion in the *Jewish War* after this brief mention. What is certain is the extraordinary impact of *Sefer Yosippon* over the following centuries, both among Jews (who read the book in communities all over the Mediterranean world, in Palestine and in Byzantium and soon in Northern Europe) and in due course also among Muslims and Christians. The Ethiopian Orthodox Church still regards the Ethiopic translation of *Sefer Yosippon* as Scripture.

The popularity of the *Sefer Yosippon* was based sometimes on the belief that it represented the Hebrew original of the *Jewish War*, and that this was the lost text to which Josephus had referred when he wrote that he was translating into Greek the account 'which I previously composed in my vernacular tongue' (1.3), a notion first found in the writings of the Islamic scholar Ibn Hazm (994–1064). The idea was nonsense, since Josephus had noted that his original version had also been for the benefit of non-Jews in Mesopotamia and it must therefore have been written in Aramaic rather than in Hebrew, but it was persistent. So, for instance, the identity of the author as Josephus was maintained by the Byzantine Jewish scholar Yehuda Mosconi in the fourteenth century: according to Mosconi, in a detailed introduction to *Sefer Yosippon*, Josephus ben Gurion was the author both of the Hebrew chronicle and of a longer Latin version intended for the Romans (presumably the literal version of the *Jewish War* which circulated in the name of Rufinus). According to Mosconi, 'Yosippon' was a diminutive form of Josephus's name, adopted out of modesty.[16]

The text of *Sefer Yosippon* to which Mosconi appended these remarks was in fact much enlarged and altered from the version in the manuscript from 953 CE, and the chronicle seems to have been frequently reworked by Jewish authors down to the fifteenth century. Before Mosconi, there had been a revised version, created by an unknown author in France on the Rhineland, which was quoted by Rashi in the eleventh century in his commentary on Daniel 5:1 and 6:29. Another version, which included parts of the Hebrew Alexander romance, was produced in the twelfth century. Such alterations of the text could be quite easily contrived because of its composite nature—it was straightforward to add to the text new material, such as the apocryphal additions to the biblical book of Daniel, without altering the structure and rhythm of the work as a whole. It must have been tempting to make such changes for those Jews who used *Yosippon* as an authority in debates with Christians on the correct interpretation of the exile and the destruction of the Temple.[17]

The popularity of *Yosippon* was demonstrated not only by frequent copying and citation but also by translations. The earliest, into Arabic (the lingua franca of much of Jewry in this period), was made already in the tenth or eleventh century. Such translations helped considerably in spreading knowledge of the work. So too did the incorporation of parts of the work into larger compilations, such as the *Sefer ha-Kabbalah* of Abraham ibn Daud (in 1161) and the massive *Chronicles of Jerahme'el*, produced by Eleazar ben Asher ha-Levi in the Rhineland in the fourteenth century as a chronological record of Jewish history from the creation of the world. The popularity of the work is easily enough explained by its utility as the only source of postbiblical Jewish history of impeccable Jewish origin because it was believed to have been composed in Hebrew. Jews were not much given to historiography as a genre, but a chronicle that explained the destruction of Jerusalem and the origins of the Jewish exile over the past millennium was of great value in the commemoration of the past that distinguished Jewish liturgy. Passages from *Yosippon* made their way into the dirges of the fast day on Ninth of Av, which commemorates the destruction of the Temple. The *Sefer Yosippon* became the most influential Hebrew historical work of the Middle Ages.[18]

Fame in the Christian World (600–1450)

For scholars in Byzantium around 600 CE the works of Josephus constituted an invaluable source for the composition of chronicles, of which many were produced between the sixth and twelfth centuries. Priests, monks, and imperial officials sought to reinforce the worldview of the Christian empire by tracing the history of the world from the creation to their own times. For John Malalas, whose *Chronographia* was completed by 565, Josephus was 'most wise', an accolade shared with other trusted sources for his history. Josephus was a particularly good witness to the destruction of Jerusalem as a 'Hebrew who was present at the war'. Malalas may well have picked up this information from another Christian source rather than from the *Jewish War* itself. The anonymous *Chronicon Paschale* includes references to Josephus's work in an extensive treatment of Second Temple Jewish history that focused on the calendar leading up to the Incarnation, the date of Easter, the life of Jesus, and the history of the early Church, but the assertion in the *Chronicon* that Josephus's fifth book on the destruction of Jerusalem explained the disaster as punishment for the death of James will have come almost certainly from Eusebius rather than directly from Josephus's own history.[19]

A renewed burst of interest in the composition of world chronicles began in Byzantium in the early ninth century, with the much more careful and critical compilation produced by George Synkellos, whose *Ekloga Chronographica* was completed in ca. 810 CE and frequently disputes the judgment of earliest Christian chronographers, particularly on contentious issues of dating. It is probable that Synkellos had access to more sources than earlier Byzantine chronographers since he was writing at the beginning of a Byzantine humanism that saw a revival of interest in the past and encouraged investigation into ancient texts. But although he seems to have made direct use of Josephus's *Antiquities* for the biblical period, the *Jewish War* was still cited by him through the filter of Eusebius. It was only with the patriarch Photius in the mid-ninth century, whose compendium, the *Bibliotheca*, recorded and described the ancient sources, including the works of Josephus, that direct engagement with the *Jewish War* in its original form can be found. By the early thirteenth century the historian Niketas Choniates was able to make an explicit reference to Josephus's depiction of Jerusalem in reference to the *Jewish War* in order to point up immoral behavior in his own time. Niketas's history of the Eastern Roman Empire stressed the consequences of impiety and the role of divine providence much as Josephus had done. The rebels and imperial troops who fought sacrilegiously within the church of Hagia Sophia in 1181 were compared unfavorably to Titus, who (according to Josephus) had tried to spare the Temple.[20]

Photius in the ninth century had rather remarkably singled out Josephus for high praise as a master of prose style, a judgment echoed some four centuries later (in ca. 1330) by the Byzantine intellectual Theodore Metochites, who discussed at length the easy flowing style to be found in Josephus's writings. It is no accident that Photius was writing at a time when Josephus's works were being copied in much greater numbers than in previous generations. We cannot know how often new copies were made of the *Jewish War* between its composition and the tenth century, but it is noteworthy that only one late third-century papyrus codex fragment (of 2.570–59, 582–84, dealing with Josephus's campaign in Galilee) survives from Egypt, in marked contrast to the numerous fragments of more popular literary works. But the seven surviving Byzantine manuscripts of Josephus's works dated from the tenth to twelfth centuries show that by this period he had become an important author worthy of the considerable trouble and expense involved in the production of a new manuscript copy. It is a remarkable fact that more manuscripts survive from this period for Josephus than for either Herodotus or Thucydides. Nor was this just a phenomenon in the imperial capital. In the second half of the fourteenth century a scribe in Astros, an obscure town in the Peloponnese, chose to copy the full text of the *Jewish War*, as well as the texts of other Greek historians (Xenophon and Herodotus). The manuscript of the *Jewish War* he copied (Barocci 151) survives in the Bodleian Library.[21]

Elsewhere in the Christian world the *Jewish War* found new readers in translation, either direct from the Greek or (more often) from the literal Latin version ascribed (misleadingly) to Rufinus. No complete translation of the book now survives in Syriac, but it may have existed at one time. Book 6, on the destruction of Jerusalem, was included at the end of the Syriac Codex Ambrosianus (721), a manuscript, containing the complete Old Testament, copied at the end of the sixth century or the start of the seventh. Passages from other parts of the *Jewish War* were quoted in a 'letter' preserved in an eighth-century manuscript, attributed to 'Sargis the Stylite of Gusit' and said to have been written 'against a Jew who argued that God has no son, and that God was not begotten.'[22]

These Syriac versions of the *Jewish War* were composed in northern Mesopotamia, in the region to which Josephus claimed to have sent the first draft of his history in Aramaic

(1.3). Syriac is a dialect of Aramaic, but there has been no suggestion that the translators were aware of any original text by Josephus apart from the Greek. The same is not true of the medieval Slavonic version, which was hailed by the Estonian scholar Alexander Berendts in the early twentieth century as an accurate representation of the Aramaic *Jewish War* on the basis of the numerous divergences between the Slavonic and the Greek texts. The claim was fiercely challenged almost as soon as it was made, not least because attempts to identify Aramaicisms in the Slavonic Josephus proved implausibly optimistic. But it remains difficult to explain all the characteristics of the Slavonic version simply as the product of faulty translation from the Greek. In the 1920s much excitement was generated when the Austrian Jewish historian Robert Eisler claimed to be able to show that the Slavonic version had been translated not from the Aramaic but from Josephus's first rough Greek version of the Aramaic before he polished up the Greek into the form found in the Greek manuscripts. But Eisler's credibility was diminished by his enthusiastic use of references to John the Baptist and Jesus in the Slavonic text to promote his own highly idiosyncratic reinterpretation of the history of early Christianity.

Eisler's theories were already generally dismissed by the mid-1930s, but the Slavonic Josephus continues to exert a certain fascination for scholars hoping to reach back to what was written by Josephus in the immediate aftermath of the war. The earliest manuscript of the *Jewish War* in Slavonic is dated to 1463 and provides no hint of the original time, place, or author of the translation. The earliest possible date for the text would be the ninth century, when a school of translators set about putting the Scriptures and other religiously

FIGURE 2.2 Josephus as a Roman. Marble bust of the Flavian era, identified with Josephus by Robert Eisler in 1930 on account of its allegedly Jewish appearance. Reproduction by permission of Ny Carlsberg Glyptotek, Copenhagen.

significant books into a dialect now known as Old Church Slavonic for the benefit of recent converts to Christianity in what is now Bulgaria. But many forms found in the Slavonic Josephus are also possible in the Old Russian dialect used by translators in Kiev, the capital of the kingdom of Rus. Rus was converted to Christianity only in the late tenth century, and dates for the Slavonic *Jewish War* as late as the fourteenth century have been mooted. There is not much evidence either in favor or against. What is certain is that the Slavonic version omits much material found in the Greek, including the prologue to book 1, and that books 2–4 (including Josephus's Galilean campaign) are presented in a much abridged form, whereas books 5–7 are translated almost in full.

Of the passages in the Slavonic text that are not in the Greek manuscripts, many can be explained as Christian additions much like those inserted by Ps.-Hegesippus into his Latin paraphrase, and some, like the details of military tactics used by Vitellius (three-pronged irons to disable Otho's horses) or vivid depictions of the sounds of battle, may reflect the military interests of the translator. But some apparently random details, such as the amount of oil used by those who perpetrated sacrilege or an illustration of the prohibition placed on the inhabitants of Jerusalem on burial of the dead by noting that even scattering earth on the dead from the sleeves of garments was forbidden, are harder to explain as a product of contemporary concerns in the world of the translator—although they could, of course, reflect nothing more than the translator's active imagination.[23]

In Western Christendom, stories from the *Jewish War* such as Jewish mothers eating their own children circulated widely from the mid-fourteenth century through dramatizations of the destruction of Jerusalem. These plays, in German, French, Italian, Spanish, English, and Latin, were staged frequently in numerous communities across Europe. But for direct access to the *Jewish War*, the Latin versions (both the Ps.-Hegesippus paraphrase and the literal translation attributed to Rufinus) served most readers as a sufficient resource without vernacular translations until late in the medieval period. There survive considerably over two hundred medieval Latin manuscripts of Josephus's works, with the *Jewish War* included in many, and references to Josephus in exegetical and historical writings abound. Marginalia in the Josephus manuscripts reveal that these were texts that were read and used. On the other hand, for Christians like Bede in England in the eighth century and for scholarly monks in the Carolingian Renaissance, who focused on standardizing the text of the Bible and on religious education in the ninth century, Josephus's *Antiquities* were his works of greatest value for elucidation of biblical history. Ps.-Hegesippus's version of the *Jewish War* was cherished as much for the Christianizing interpretation of the destruction of Jerusalem imposed on Josephus's text by the fourth-century translation as for Josephus's original narrative.[24]

That the flurry of Latin manuscripts of Josephus copied in the ninth century was followed by a gap in the late tenth and early eleventh centuries reflects a general trend in the copying of Latin writings in general. Hence the majority of the manuscripts of Josephus date to the twelfth and thirteenth centuries, when Josephus came to be used as a matter of course along with patristic texts as a guide to biblical study. Many of these Latin manuscripts were richly decorated, often using the same artistic motifs as in manuscripts of the New Testament for subject matter found also in the *Jewish War*, but occasionally focusing on themes unique to Josephus.

Among the unique illustrations are depictions of Josephus himself, and these are quite revealing of continuing ambiguity with regard to the author's status in a Christian world. A miniature in a Latin manuscript of the *Jewish War* from the ninth century, which portrays an oriental messenger in Parthian dress with a soldier's helmet and herald's wand, identified him in Greek as 'Josephus the Historian'. A portrait in the prologue of a Latin text of the *Jewish War* from ca. 1130 depicts him, like a biblical prophet, as a richly attired and bearded figure in twelfth-century costume holding an open book (displaying the *Testimonium Flavianum*) and confronted by a seated scribe, portrayed as a tonsured monk.

In a Latin manuscript of the *Antiquities* written in the Weingarten monastery rather later in the twelfth century, Josephus is shown at the head of a group of Jews wearing the standard Jew's hat of the twelfth century, and writing on a long roll that he is portrayed as presenting to Vespasian (who is in turn depicted as a Christian emperor). At the beginning of book 7 of the *Jewish War* in another twelfth-century manuscript, Josephus fixes a stern gaze on Mary eating her child and points to her with his left hand, as he stands next to her on the battlement of Jerusalem and Titus advances on the city on a horse and with sword drawn— Josephus is thus portrayed as both participant and witness to the most terrible event of the war.[25]

The fame of Josephus was thus spread throughout Christendom in the Middle Ages, even if his works were known in different forms and languages. The fables of Aesop in Syriac were attributed to Josephus, and legends about Josephus as a physician who had cured Titus can be found in the *Sachsenspiegel* in medieval Germany. Contemporary conflicts from the struggles in Kievan Rus in the tenth century to the ambitions of crusaders reflected in Anglo-Norman historiography and the impact of the sack of Constantinople in 1204 added

FIGURE 2.3 Josephus as a biblical prophet with a monk as a scribe. Historiated initial 'C' in the prologue of a manuscript of a Latin translation of the *Jewish War* (Cambridge, ca. 1130). Reproduction by permission of the Master and Fellows of St John's College, Cambridge.

piquancy and relevance to Josephus's account of the fall of Jerusalem. But the fame and influence of the *Jewish War* were to grow even more as the fall of Byzantium in 1453 brought a flood of Greek knowledge and manuscripts from the Greek world to the Latin West.[26]

Rediscovery of the Greek Book (1450–1750)

CHAPTER 3

Christians 1450–1750

For Christian humanist scholars of Italy in the second half of the fifteenth century, access to this new learning lay above all through mastery of the languages of the East—first, and most obviously, Greek and then (increasing in the sixteenth century) Hebrew. An explosion of printing, particularly by presses in Italy and Germany, brought the discoveries of these scholars to the attention of an enlarged reading public across Europe. Books unknown outside the Greek-speaking world were rediscovered, plumbed for their ancient wisdom, and popularized. Among the most exciting of the new discoveries were the writings of the Jewish Greek authors of antiquity, Josephus's original Greek works among them.

But the reception of the Greek version of the *Jewish War* in the early modern period was shaped by the need to adapt the new discoveries to the established reputation of Josephus as known through the Latin translations. Josephus was already famous. Thus in the early decades of the Renaissance, the Italian humanist scholar Gugleimo Raimondo Moncada adopted in Rome in 1481 the name 'Flavius Mithridates' in honor of Flavius Josephus. It seems that he saw

Josephus as a role model, thus neatly denoting his own status as an exotically oriental Jew (albeit actually from Sicily) who had become part of mainstream Roman society. Mithridates, who had converted to Christianity, belonged in the interstices between the Jewish and Christian worlds. He is best known as the supplier to Giovanni Pico della Mirandola of the Latin versions of kabbalistic texts that enabled Pico to establish his controversial claims about the high value of the Kabbalah for Christians.[1]

The first printed edition of the *Jewish War* in Greek appeared in Basel in 1544 at the Froben press. Quite a few other Greek texts were printed for the first time only in the 1540s and 1550s, so the date is not wholly surprising. But many other Greek writings had been published in print over the past half century, and the delay in production of a Greek Josephus is most easily explained by the ready availability of printed Latin versions. One edition of the old Latin translation of Josephus's works from Augsburg dates to 1470, and there were six further printings before 1500. The *Jewish War* was printed on its own in a Latin translation at least three times before the end of the fifteenth century. Manuscripts of the Greek text were to be found in fifteenth-century Italy, but they were hard to access and there is not much evidence of an interest among scholars in examining the Greek until well into the sixteenth century. Even then, the Greek manuscript of the *Jewish War* to which Erasmus referred in a letter of 30 January 1533 was being used by the publishing house Froben as an aid to improve the text of the late-antique Latin translation that it was printing.[2]

The *editio princeps* of 1544 required a great deal of scholarly work by the editors in the printing house. The editor

Arlenius collected manuscripts from a variety of sources as the basis of his text, which covered all the works of Josephus in the order frequently found in manuscripts—that is, the *Antiquities* (with the *Life* appended), followed by the *Jewish War*, and *Against Apion* at the end. One of the manuscripts used had been copied in Venice in 1542 and was presumably ordered from a copyist for the edition, but two other manuscripts used by Arlenius (and now in Schleusingen) had been copied some twenty or thirty years earlier. The marginal notes still to be seen on these manuscripts reveal the extensive intervention required by the printers as editors in order to achieve a coherent text. Some marks simply indicate the start of new chapters in the printed edition, but others frequently correct the Greek, demonstrating an extraordinarily impressive command of the language.[3]

The decision to produce the first printed edition placed the study of Josephus firmly in the mainstream of humanist scholarship—the first editions of Eusebius's *Ecclesiastical History* and *Praeparatio Evangelica* came out in the same year (in Paris). Arlenius's edition would prove to be long-lasting. In part this was because the size of the undertaking to print all of Josephus's writings was too daunting for later scholars. But it was also significant that by the second half of the seventeenth century, a hundred years after Arlenius, the motivation for a new edition of Josephus to be produced in Oxford at the recently founded University Press was not so much classical antiquity as the history of Judaism in the context of the early Church. Thus in 1672 John Fell, the bishop of Oxford, included plans to print in Oxford editions of Josephus in Greek and Latin alongside biblical texts (in Greek, Aramaic, and Coptic), as well as Greek, Latin, and Syriac patristic texts, and the *Mishneh Torah* of Maimonides. The task was assigned to Edward Bernard (1638–97), who was professor of astronomy in Oxford and an expert on oriental languages. He was able to make use (after considerable diplomatic negotiation) of variant readings culled from Josephus manuscripts from all over Europe that had been collected by Johan Andreas Bosius (1626–74), professor of history at Jena; the manuscripts specifically of the *Jewish War* used by Bosius came from Leipzig and Wroclaw, and Bernard added further variants from manuscripts in England (including the Bodleian library). The problem was that visits to libraries kept adding more and more variant readings, and the closer that Bernard looked into rabbinic texts the more he found he could add to his notes on the *Antiquities* to demonstrate his scholarship. Frustrated by the delay, the Press in Oxford published an edition of book 1 and part of book 2 of the *Jewish War* in 1687 under the editorship of Henry Aldrich (1647–1710), the dean of Christ Church, with a full array of the variant readings of the Greek manuscripts but no notes to draw attention to the variants in the Latin and parallels in rabbinic literature. The choice of the books of the *Jewish War* for publication rather than other writings by Josephus may have been encouraged precisely by the lack of pertinent rabbinic material with which to burden the text.[4]

The question of Josephus's relationship to rabbinic literature was not trivial for these scholars, who debated intensively whether he should be understood primarily in relationship to the Greek Bible (i.e., the Septuagint) or the masoretic text used by rabbinic Jews. The issue concerned predominantly the interpretation of Josephus's *Antiquities*, but it emerged also in an emendation of a passage of the *Jewish War* by the great scholar Casaubon (1559–1614). Josephus described, at 7.98–99, the Sambation river, which flows on the Sabbath and is dry for the rest of the week. This view was contradicted by the medieval Jewish commentator Elijah Levita, who asserted that the river flows for the rest of the week and runs dry on Saturdays. Where Casaubon in 1614 dealt with the contradiction by emending the text of Josephus to bring his account into line with the rabbis, the Dutch scholar Isaac Vossius in the 1660s and 1670s saw Josephus's text, here and elsewhere, as testimony to a Jewish Greek tradition radically at odds with the rabbis and much to be preferred. The full edition of Josephus's works eventually printed by Oxford University Press was edited by the classicist John Hudson, who was librarian of the Bodleian Library from 1701 to his death in 1719. Hudson's edition, published posthumously in 1720 by his friend the antiquarian Anthony Hall, was a far less complex production than Bernard had envisaged, with textual variants simply noted. A rival edition by the Dutch classicist Sisebert Haverkamp followed in 1726 but does not seem to have been widely circulated.[5]

It should not be imagined that these scholarly issues had much impact on the life of the *Jewish War* among the general Christian populace. Even those able to read the Greek often preferred to read the book in the familiar Latin version or in one of the many vernacular translations widely available in printed form. Already before 1500, translations into Spanish, Catalan, French, and Italian were to be found in print.

The timing of the publication of the Spanish version by Alfonso de Palencia at the very end of his life, on 27 March

FIGURE 3.1 Fighting within Jerusalem during the siege. Miniature
from a manuscript of a French translation of the *Jewish War* (Paris,
1492). Courtesy of Bibliothèque Nationale, Paris (VELINS-696,
p. CXXXIVr).

1492, four days before the expulsion edict of Queen Isabella
(to whom the work is dedicated, on the grounds that Josephus's history shows the divine punishment of the Jews), is
unlikely to have been an accident, especially when the *Jewish
War* was published along with the defense of Judaism in

Against Apion (unlike the French edition of the same year and the Italian of 1494, in which the *Jewish War* was presented alone). In Spain the book served to remind Spaniards about the Sephardic culture they were about to expel (and by which they would remain haunted over ensuing centuries in a hunt for traces of Judaizing among those left behind). The drive behind a rash of publications of the *Jewish War* in French in the second half of the sixteenth century owed most to perceived parallels between the internecine battles in Jerusalem described by Josephus and the wars of religion which threatened divine vengeance on France. A similar motive may be surmised for the publication of no fewer than seven vernacular editions of the *Jewish War* in the war-torn Netherlands in the sixteenth century. The first English translation by the physician, author, and playwright Thomas Lodge was published only in 1602. Advertised as the 'Famous and Memorable works of Josephus, a man of much honour and learning among the Jews', the translation appeared more as an academic and scholarly work than as a reaction to contemporary events, despite Lodge's adventurous life, in which he had been to sea and traveled as far as Brazil.[6]

None of these vernacular versions of the book made use of the Greek text, despite the availability of manuscripts and the efforts of Arlenius in 1544; Thomas Lodge's translation was derived specifically from the Latin and the French. But in the course of the seventeenth century attempts to produce new translations based on the Greek are testimony to increasing awareness that the Greek text might be more authentic. A new French translation from the Greek by Arnauld D'Andilly, published in 1667, was claimed as the basis of an anonymous version of Lodge printed in 1676 (although the revisions to the original were actually minimal). Claims to have used the Greek appear in the ensuing English versions by Roger L'Estrange in 1692 and H. Jackson in 1732. They can also be found, most influentially, in the translation in 1737 by William Whiston, former Lucasian Professor of Mathematics at Cambridge, which was presented as made from the 'original Greek, according to Haverkamp's accurate edition'.

Whiston's translation was to enjoy exceptional popularity, partly because of the considerable reputation of the translator as a scholar and religious polemicist. His historical studies persuaded him of the need to promote a version of primitive Christianity, rejecting the Trinitarian Nicene creed and encouraging literal acceptance of biblical accounts of the miraculous and prophecy. Deprived of his university post and barred from any role in the Anglican Church, he made a living as a lecturer on scientific and religious topics in London, energetically engaging in controversy on mathematics and chronology as much as theology up to his death, aged eighty-four, in 1752. The success of his Josephus translation may have owed as much to his popularization of the *Antiquities* and the polemical essays attached to the translation as to his rendering of the *Jewish War*.[7]

Printers of these vernacular versions of Josephus's book often sought to capture the attention of potential purchasers through lurid illustrations on the title page. The Dutch translation of 'all of the works of Flavius Josephus' by Willem Sewel in 1704 portrays Judaea as a maid in chains, gazing in horror at the Temple in flames as 'the most dreadful punishment, the consequence of grave sins, is visited upon the Jewish state'.

FIGURE 3.2 The capture of Jerusalem. Title page of a printed
edition of a Dutch translation of Josephus's works (Amsterdam,
1704). Photo, courtesy of the University of Michigan.

The frontispiece was all-important in selling the book and seems to have been considered worthy of much more attention and expense than the illustrations within the text, which were often recycled by the printers from other works (including Bibles). One striking innovation was the use of the plural ('The Jewish Wars') in many of the English editions, starting with Thomas Lodge in 1602. The practice is also found in some other translations, such as a Castilian edition in 1557, which has 'las guerras de los Judios'. The plural has no justification in Josephus's own name for his history or in the Latin—apart from errors by modern scholars, the only reference to the work as *Bella Judaica* I have been able to find is a learned article on the river Sambatyon by a certain Rabbi Moses Edrahi in *Fraser's Magazine*, published in London in 1837.[8]

It is tempting to explain the focus on the internal strife of the Jews as a reflection of the internal divisions within European Christian society in the sixteenth and seventeenth centuries, with the implicit warning that such divisiveness could incur divine wrath on Christendom as it had once done for the Jews. The destruction of Jerusalem was a popular topic in Church liturgy: the *Jewish War* was being read on Good Fridays in Leipzig in the eighteenth century when Johann Sebastian Bach composed the *St John Passion* to add to the service. In England, the topic was picked by Protestants in the sixteenth and seventeenth centuries in ballads and puppet shows in London and the provinces. The message from both preachers and actors that 'Jerusalem's destruction is a warning for England' and that the time is ripe for repentance evinced an empathy for the Jewish suffering depicted quite different from the gloating about the punishment of the Jews found in much Christian literature in late antiquity and the Middle Ages. At the same time, Josephus's book provided material for entertainment as well as moral instruction and proved popular as a source for Jacobean playwrights—hence a play (now lost) called *Titus and Vespasian* (performed in 1592), Elizabeth Cary's *Tragedy of Mariam* (composed ca. 1604), a play called *Herod and Antipater* written by Gervase Markham and William Sampson in ca. 1613, and William Heminge's *The Jewes Tragedy*, which was composed in ca. 1626 but printed only in 1662, the year when Jews were permitted to return to England under Oliver Cromwell.[9]

The printed text of *The Jewes Tragedy*, which depicts the treachery and subsequent downfall of three seditious Jewish captains during the assault on Jerusalem by Nero and 'Vespatian', advertises the dependence of the story on the 'Authentick and Famous History of JOSEPHUS'. Josephus himself appears as the character Joseph who defects to the Romans early in the play and becomes the hero of the drama. Whether the audience would have connected the character in the play with the author of the history is less certain: no direct link is made in the wording of the play, but if the original performance in the 1620s was at Heminge's college in Oxford, which was Christ Church, perhaps he could assume that they would have known enough about Josephus not to need to be told. Markham and Sampson's *Herod and Antipater* is a play of passion and villainy with much depiction of violence and bloodshed in dumb show as well as in the words. Josephus appears as a choral figure drawing attention to the moral significance of these events, as in his description of Antipater (II.1.630–63),

Never grew Pride more high, more desperate;
Nor ever could the Arrogance of man
Finde out a Breast more large and spacious.

Josephus the writer had been introduced to the audience in the Prologue, which proclaimed that 'IOSEPHUS'
th'Ancient Writer, with a Pen//Lent by the Muses, gives
new life to Men', but the audience is not informed that the
narrator is the same Josephus, presumably because ordinary
playgoers did not know enough about Josephus to care
about the identity of the chorus narrator. Insistence on Josephus's learning and fame in the printed version of the play
appealed to the more sophisticated tastes of the literate public, who would be impressed by the historical credentials of
both author and narrator.

Heminge and his audience could easily have known the
Jewish War through the translation by Thomas Lodge,
which had been published first in 1602 and was frequently
reprinted, but—ironically in light of this emphasis on Josephus's authority—in fact his source was not a translation
into English of the Latin version of Josephus's original
Greek but an abridged version in English of a Latin version
of the Hebrew Yosippon: Peter Morwen's *History of the
Latter Times of the Jewes Commune Weale*. Morwen's history was reprinted thirteen times between its first publication in 1558 and 1615 and served as the most common introduction to Josephus for ordinary readers. The enthusiastic
reception of Yosippon by some Christian readers is one of
the more surprising aspects of the life of the *Jewish War* in
early modern Europe. In *The Jewes Tragedy*, dependence on
Yosippon is clear enough from the list of characters in the

play, which includes one 'Joseph son of Gorion and Captain of the Jews'.[10]

Heminge's awareness of the existence of the *Sefer Yosippon* can be traced to the publication of the text with a Latin translation in Basel in 1541 by Sebastian Münster, three years before the first edition of Josephus's original Greek was printed for the first time in the same city. Münster, originally a Franciscan, had accepted an appointment in the university in Basel in 1529 and devoted himself to the study of Hebrew. Among other works he published an edition of the Hebrew Bible with a Latin translation in 1534–35, and a Hebrew version of the gospel of Matthew in 1537. His interest in *Sefer Yosippon* probably lay in the assumption that the Hebrew text of a Jewish writing must be more authentic than the text in Greek.[11]

Münster's Latin version had been anticipated by a partial translation of Yosippon in Castilian as early as 1461–80, but it was from Münster that Peter Morwen derived his English version, published in 1558. The rapid reception of Münster's work in England was probably not accidental—Münster had dedicated his Hebrew Gospel of Matthew to Henry VIII, who was seen as a champion of the new knowledge embraced by the reformers. At the start of the seventeenth century the great Genevan classical scholar Isaac Casaubon, who spent most of his life in France and moved to England only in his last years, at one point set out himself to translate *Sefer Yosippon* into Latin and abandoned the project only on discovering Münster's bilingual edition. He noted on the title page of his copy of Münster that the great Hebraist had been wrong in his notion that Yosippon was the original from which the Greek *Jewish War* was translated. But he reckoned that the mistake had been understandable, since 'when we read the book of Joseph Ben Gorion, we perceived that the author spoke about himself in such a confused way towards the end of the first book that it would be reasonable for anyone to be led into error by him'.[12]

For Casaubon, as for Joseph Justus Scaliger, a French scholar (also a Huguenot) from the previous generation, demonstrating the accuracy of the *Jewish War* in its full Greek form had the advantage that it put Josephus's prestige on the side of Protestants in a long-running dispute with Catholic historians about the origins of monasticism. Catholics like Cesare Baronio had claimed that the Essenes, described by Josephus, constituted early forms of Christian monasticism, a notion derived ultimately from Epiphanius and Jerome in the fourth century CE. The Greek version of Josephus's excursus on the Essenes seemed to prove this theory wrong. Both Scaliger and Casaubon protested also against Baronio's preference for the later testimony of Jerome and Eusebius over that of the contemporary Jew Josephus regarding the heavenly voices heard in Jerusalem before the Temple was destroyed. Casaubon saw Josephus as a superb historian of the Jewish war. He scrutinized his text for political lessons and commented with approval on his insight that in the siege of Jotapata the rationing of the water supply and the inability of the inhabitants of the town to control it were harder to bear than the thirst itself, noting that 'experience shows that this statement is true'. On Josephus's account of his speech against suicide at Jotapata, with the argument that all beings, by nature, wish to live, Casaubon noted in the margin that this was a 'golden place' (*locus aureus*) in the text. For Joseph Scaliger, Josephus's witness in book 6 of the *Jewish War* to a comet heralding the destruction of Jerusalem was a key component of an ingenious argument for solving problems in New Testament chronology by explaining the nature of the star seen seven decades earlier by the Magi at the time of Jesus's nativity.[13]

The enthusiasm of Scaliger and Casaubon for Josephus's authority as a historian was widely shared by Protestant Christians at the end of the early modern period. The *Jewish War* in Dutch was a best seller in the Dutch Republic in the eighteenth century. In 1706–7 a Huguenot intellectual, Jacques Basnage, published in Rotterdam for a Christian audience an immensely popular history of the religion of the Jews in six volumes that presented itself as a continuation of Josephus's history. Published originally in France, Basnage's *Histoire des Juifs depuis Jesus Christ jusqu'à' present*, appeared in English already in 1708. In England, Basnage's younger contemporary, William Whiston, even contrived, in the first of the Dissertations attached to his translation, to claim that Josephus was not just a Christian but also a bishop of the Ebionite Church in Jerusalem.

It is somewhat puzzling that Josephus's reception seems to have been unaffected in such circles by the availability of his *Life*, with all its contradictions of the *Jewish War*'s account of his political career and his role as rebel commander in Galilee that have so much troubled more recent readers. The *Life* had not been translated into Latin in late antiquity along with the *Antiquities*, and it was therefore unknown in Western Christendom until the Renaissance, but it was often included in the early modern translations of Josephus's works into vernacular languages. Apparently it was not always read with much attention.

A letter sent to a friend by the evangelical hymn writer William Cowper in 1783 provides a glimpse into both the popularity of Josephus's works for a general readership and the glimmerings of a new skepticism. Cowper wrote to the Rev. William Unwin on 24 November of that year:

> L'Estrange's Josephus has lately furnished us with evening lectures. But the historian is so tediously circumstantial and the translator so insupportably coarse and vulgar, that we are all three weary of him. How would Tacitus have shone upon such a subject, great master as he was of the art of description, concise without obscurity, and affecting without being poetical. But so it was ordered, and for wise reasons, no doubt, that the greatest calamities any people ever suffered, and an accomplishment of one of the most signal prophecies in the Scripture, should be recorded by one of the worst writers.

Cowper was a poet, and his complaints about Josephus's literary style reflect the taste of the age, but it is curious that the translation to which he was subjected was the 1692 version by Roger L'Estrange rather than Whiston's translation of 1737, which had already been reprinted many times. If Cowper objected to Whiston on religious principle, he could have turned to one of a number of translations that had been published since 1737 in competition, such as the edition by James Wilson published in London in 1740 or the joint translation by Ebenezer Thompson and William Charles Price printed in 1777. Such new versions were often commissioned by subscribers who undertook to purchase a copy—836, in the case of the Thompson and Price translation, and 396 for the rival version by Charles Clarke, which appeared in 1785 and must have been in preparation when Cowper wrote. Publication of two further English editions within a few years—by George Maynard in 1789 and by Thomas Bradshaw in 1792—confirms the vibrancy of interest in reading Josephus's works in a readable and reliable form.[14]

But William Cowper's letter went on to make a complaint about Josephus that seems to be novel in Christian attitudes to the historian. He wrote to Unwin that 'the man was a temporizer too, and courted the favor of his Roman masters at the expense of his own creed, or else an infidel and absolutely disbelieved it'. Such attacks on the personal integrity of the historian foreshadow the arguments about Josephus and the *Jewish War* in the following century, but among Jews rather than Christians.

Jews 1450–1750

Back at the start of the early modern period, for a Jew like the historiographer Azariah de'Rossi (1511–77) there was no cause to express such concerns about the morality of the author of the *Jewish War*. Simply the discovery of the Greek Josephus, which had for so long been ignored within rabbinic Judaism, was a delight:

> Now our blessed God has granted the people of our times to become acquainted with the writers of antiquity who wrote in their own context, and with authors whose works have laid hidden and interred, undetected by our people. It is as though they had become completely obliterated: for

they were written in the Greek script and language and
were therefore inaccessible to the assemblies of our later
sages of blessed memory.

Azariah himself knew little Greek, and the *Jewish War* he got
to know was a Latin translation of the Greek, either in the
version attributed to Rufinus and edited by the Christian humanist Segismund Gelenius, printed in Basel in 1534, or in
Gelenius's own independent translation, which was published in 1548 and reprinted a number of times. The problem
for Azariah and his Jewish readers was to establish the relationship between this Latin text, long known to their Christian compatriots and treated by them as authoritative, and
Sefer Yosippon, which, by Azariah's time, had been enshrined
in Jewish liturgy and folk memory over many centuries.[15]

To be sure, already in the fifteenth century the Jewish
Portuguese statesman and philosopher Isaac ben Judah
Abravanel had distinguished between what he considered
to be the works of Josephus written for Jews in Hebrew
(that is, Yosippon) and the writings of Josephus addressed
to the Romans in Latin and Greek. But for Abravanel this
was not taken to imply the superiority of either text, and
for much of the early modern period many Jews treated
both the Greek and the Hebrew versions as authentic. Yosippon became if anything even more popular among the
Jews in precisely this period, first through the printing of
the Hebrew text (first undertaken in Mantua between
1476 and 1479) and then through dissemination of a Yiddish version by Michael Adam first published in 1546 'for
merchants who do not have time to study Torah'. The title
page of a Yiddish *Yosippon* from the early eighteenth

century proclaims it as 'a book about wonderful things, [relating] what happened to our ancestors during the Second Temple, how they prospered and succeeded in all their wars. And it also explains the Temple building, [and] its great glory, the high status of the kings of Israel until the end of the destruction of the Temple'. Much of the triumphalist narrative thus advertised (somewhat selectively, of course) had been taken by the author of *Sefer Yosippon* not from the *Jewish War* but from Josephus's *Antiquities*, but that is not something that readers of the Yiddish book would have known. It is easy to see why this positive presentation of Jewish history was so popular. Despite the incorporation in *Sefer Yosippon* of much of Ps.-Hegesippus's version of the *Jewish War*, the illustrated frontispiece of the printed publication of the Yiddish Yosippon notably eschewed the moral teachings about the destruction of Jerusalem as the consequence of sin that had been emphasized in his Christian source material.[16]

Indeed the popularity of Yosippon among Ashkenazi Jews down to the mid-eighteenth century and beyond can be gauged from the use of his name to gain a readership for a remarkable publishing venture by the Amsterdam scholar Menachem Man ben Shlomo haLevi Amelander for his continuation of Jewish history from 70 CE down to his own times. The words printed on the title page in large bold letters were 'of Sefer Yosippon', with 'the second part' printed above in smaller letters and the actual title of the book (*Sheyris Israel*, 'The Remnant of Israel') in smaller letters still. The presentation of new historical works as a continuation of classic histories from which the new material can borrow authority had been common since antiquity, not least in the successor histories appended to Eusebius's *Ecclesiastical History*. But Amelander was strikingly humble in his references to himself as 'an ordinary man' (*ayn gemainer man*) in comparison to Yosef ben Gurion haKohen, who had been a mighty man, a warrior, and *hasid* ('pious'). Amelander claimed that he sought to imitate his great predecessor only in his love for truth and his willingness to use non-Jewish sources when Jewish evidence was lacking. There was nothing accidental about this praise for Yosippon in a publishing project specifically designed, according to Amelander's preface, to displace for observant Ashkenazi Jews books full of 'idleness and lies' by providing them with instructive, edifying reading in their leisure time and to encourage a conviction that the end of exile and the restoration of the Temple were imminent. Amelander did not make it explicit for his Yiddish readers, but the polemic had a very specific target in Basnage's history of the religion of the Jews that had appeared in Dutch in an abridgement in 1719 and then in full in 1726 and had become, in the eyes of Amelander, much too popular as reading for Dutch Jews.[17]

Basnage's primary interest had been in a Christian reading public, but the list of subscribers to the 1726 edition included a number of prominent Sephardi Jews from the Amsterdam community. For many of these Sephardim Josephus was familiar in Latin or another language from the Catholic culture they had known in the Iberian Peninsula as conversos. At least two of them had themselves attempted unsuccessfully a continuation of Jewish history 'from Flavius Josephus to our times', as Basnage had freely acknowledged. One of these Sephardim was Menasseh ben Israel, the rabbi and printer who was to petition Oliver Cromwell for the return of Jews to England. Such sophisticated Sephardi intellectuals shared with Protestants like Basnage an admiration for the 'Graeco-Latin' Josephus. But they parted company in their evaluation of the *Sefer Yosippon*. Basnage, in the tradition of critical Humanist scholarship, had attacked the traditional rabbinic view that the author, Yosef ben Gurion, was to be equated with Flavius Josephus, and he had built on the research of Scaliger and others to suggest that *Yosippon* was composed by a French rabbi, probably from Bretagne, at the end of the tenth or eleventh century. Such an assault on the authenticity of a work held in high esteem by Jews was strongly opposed by Menasseh ben Israel, who insisted firmly in a letter in French to Christopher Arnold on 6 December 1651 that *Yosippon* was just as authentic as the Greek *Jewish War*:

> There is no doubt that Flavius Josephus, it is certain, has always been constant in the Jewish religion, of the Pharisee sect; as he witnesses himself at the start of his Life, which he wrote at the end of his History . . . and at Chapter 8 of the 7th book of the Jewish War. In truth he never changed or vacillated up to his death: for the gentiles and Jews would never have forgotten to reproach him, being his capital and mortal enemies because of his close relationship with Vespasian as he shows in his testimony at Chapter 4 of book 7 of the Jewish War. . . . Touching Flavius Josephus written in Hebrew, many doubt it, including the very learned and celebrated Gerard Vossius. However, that never comes into question among us, because we believe unanimously that Flavius Josephus is the author of it.[18]

Amelander in 1743 evidently took the same view as Menasseh, nearly a century earlier. He made no attempt to deal with the critical comments of Basnage and others about *Yo-sippon* but simply reasserted the traditional view about the authenticity of the book and then—remarkably—relied on the prestige of *Yosippon* to provide authority for his use of other books by 'Yosippon to the Romans', who he supposed to be the same author:

> One should know that the name of the author of this book was Yosef ben Gurion ha-Kohen; he wrote the book in the sacred language and called it *Yosippon*, because he wanted to make his name small, which shows that he was a great pious man. . . . He also wrote a very large book in Latin, named *Yosefus*; this was translated much later into various languages and also into Dutch, and all the nations consider it a mighty book.

Amelander's history, which was reprinted frequently in the following century, thus paved the way among the Yiddish-speaking Jews of Eastern Europe for acceptance of Josephus's *Jewish War* in its original Greek form, while using Christian admiration for 'Yosefus' to convince Jewish readers of the importance of *Yosippon*. Appreciation of *Yosippon* among such readers was enhanced by the wide availability of the Yiddish translation by Michael Adam, which was reprinted twice in the seventeenth century and again (in a revised version) in Amsterdam in 1743. In the Sephardi world, a younger contemporary of Amelander, Abraham ben Isaac Asa, provided a parallel service for readers of Ladino (Judeo-Spanish). Asa was a great scholar who translated the Bible and works of Jewish law, ethics, and science into Judeo-Spanish in an attempt, with a circle of intellectual colleagues in Istanbul, to raise the spiritual level of the Jews of the

Ottoman Empire. In 1753 he published a Ladino version of *Sefer Yosippon*.[19]

Evidently the reputation of Josephus among Jews was very high as the eighteenth century drew to a close. This had little to do with the use of the *Antiquities* as confirmation of the biblical tradition, as among Christian Humanist scholars, nor was it entirely based on the *Jewish War* and *Yosippon*. For a brief period in the seventeenth century, the most celebrated of Josephus's works, at least among the Spanish and Portuguese Jews of Amsterdam, was not either of these historical writings but the apologetic treatise *Against Apion*, with its defense of Jewish customs and depiction of the Jewish constitution as the perfect 'theocracy'.[20]

The *haskamah* (note of approval) by Isaac Aboab da Fonseco, the leader of the Amsterdam Sephardi community, attached to a new translation of *Against Apion* into Spanish published in the city in 1687, hailed the work of 'our famous Josephus' as beneficial for 'the revelation of the God-fearing, and his Sacred Glory, and the honor of his Divine Laws, and praise of those who are observant'. Ex-conversos in Amsterdam had attained a high level of education in Latin and (sometimes) Greek in Spain or Portugal before their removal to safety in the Dutch Republic. Josephus was familiar to them from the classical curriculum in Iberian universities and must have presented a more familiar aspect in learning about their Jewish identity than rabbinic tomes in Hebrew and Aramaic. It is also probable that Josephus's position, straddling Jewish, Greek, and Roman cultures, resonated for Western Sephardim who felt themselves to be in a similarly ambiguous position. *Against Apion* was of particular interest for those in the Amsterdam community like

Menasseh ben Israel who kept in close touch with the concerns of Christian Hebraists, for whom the text was an obsession in the search for a 'Hebrew Republic', a divinely inspired polity fusing Christian sacred history with pagan political philosophy.[21]

Menasseh ben Israel noted in 1656 that he had a Hebrew version of *Against Apion* 'ready for the Presse', but the plan to publish it seems to have been dropped, probably because he decided that he would not find a market for it. Menasseh was deeply engaged in the book trade and must have known that a Hebrew version (published by the historian Samuel Shullam in Istanbul toward the end of the previous century) already existed, albeit attributed not to Josephus but to Yosef haKohen ben Gurion, the author of the *Sefer Yosippon*. His plan to issue another version in Hebrew suggests a desire to promote the status of the work among fellow Jews so that they could appreciate its worth as much as his Christian Hebraist friends. This would hardly have been a practical matter of making the book easier for Amsterdam Sephardim to read—for that purpose, translation into Spanish or Portuguese would have been far more appropriate. Menasseh's aim seems rather to have been to claim a place for *Against Apion* in the canon of religious writings recognized by Jews worldwide.[22]

None of the early modern Jewish readers of Josephus's works seem to have noticed the glaring discrepancy between Josephus's assertion in *Against Apion* that Jews 'have a perfect uniformity of belief', as a result of which 'all think alike about God and follow the same practices', and the description of Judaism as divided into three philosophies that he wrote about in the *Jewish War* (2.119–66) and then reiterated in the *Antiquities* and the *Life*. Jews, like Christians, picked from each source the material to their advantage. Thus, Josephus's contrast between Pharisees, Sadducees, and Essenes was co-opted for religious polemic within the Sephardi community in Amsterdam by the skeptic Uriel da Costa in his *Examination of Pharisaic Traditions*, published in Portuguese in 1623. He identified the rabbis as Pharisees, with rabbinic belief in the immortality of the soul as a devious Pharisaic invention, and authentic Judaism as the religion of the Sadducees, who had been in Josephus's time 'a minority comprising the most important, learned, and noble part of the people'.[23]

Da Costa, born to converso parents ca. 1585, had been educated in Portugal as a Catholic. He took on his Jewish name only in 1614, when he escaped Portugal and settled in Hamburg as a trader. He joined the Jewish community but rapidly became disenchanted with the form of Judaism they were practicing. By 1623, when he moved to Amsterdam, he was already a known heretic who had been subjected to a ban by the Jews of Hamburg. But he had also already been deeply engaged in polemical exchanges with Leon of Modena, a distinguished rabbi in Venice who had been called on by the Hamburg Jews to condemn his views. The two hundred pages of his *Examination of Pharisaic Traditions*, which stressed the discrepancies between the Bible and rabbinic practices, relied primarily on a combination of scripture and reason. But it was evidently important to him that his Jewish readers could be expected to recognize the authority of Josephus as testimony that his views had been shared by an important section of the Jewish community at the end of the Second Temple period.

None of these Jews seem to have been perturbed by Josephus's alleged lack of political integrity as William Cowper had been. Perhaps, in light of their own rather vulnerable positions in society, they failed to see the wickedness in being a 'temporizer' that so offended the earnest evangelical. Those able to gain access to one of the vernacular translations of Josephus's works, or one of the printed editions of the Latin, could now read Josephus's own tortuous justifications of his career in the *Life* and compare it to the vainglorious account in the *Jewish War*. But Menasseh ben Israel, who, in his letter to Arnold, referred explicitly to Josephus's self-description in the *Life*, saw in it only confirmation of Josephus's constant fidelity to Judaism. It would require a major change in the position of Jews in Europe from the end of the eighteenth century, and major developments in their self-perception in the early years of the nineteenth, before some Jews began to dismiss the *Jewish War* as the work of a traitor to his people.

Controversy

CHAPTER 4

Doubts about Josephus

One of the earliest expressions of doubt about Josephus's moral character came not from a fellow Jew but from the great Protestant theologian Edward Reuss, one of the pioneers of historical exegesis of the Bible and an early proponent of the documentary hypothesis about the origins of the Pentateuch. In his entry on Josephus (vol. 31, published in 1855) in the multivolume *Allgemeine Encyclopädie der Wissenchaften und Künste*, a massive (and, in the end, uncompleted) enterprise published piecemeal over seventy years from 1818, Reuss presented Josephus as a patriot who had contrived to remain moderate during the bitter faction fighting of a political revolution. Reuss had lived as a German-speaking Alsatian in French Strasbourg through the Napoleonic Wars and the failed revolution of 1830 and 1848, and he showed considerable empathy for Josephus. But he could not approve of Josephus's revelation to Vespasian about the divine plan that he would become emperor, noting, 'A patriot, a true Pharisee, in the good sense of the word, would never have laid down the eternal hopes of his people at the feet of the strangler of his fatherland. This one action, which he recounts with cynical smugness, without feeling any shame . . . reveals a lack of character ("Charakter-lösigkeit"), which might hold the key to Josephus' actions and writings'.[1]

But it was among Jews that Josephus's character was to come under the most intense scrutiny for much of the nineteenth and twentieth centuries, as his political and cultural role in relation to Rome was reevaluated in light of the possibilities of Jewish emancipation and integration into wider society opening up across Western Europe. Napoleon in 1806 offered Jews the opportunity to become fully French so long as their Jewish identity was confined to their private and domestic lives. As other European states over the nineteenth century made similar offers of partial emancipation to their Jewish subjects, and the entry of Jews into mainstream European society sparked an anti-Semitic backlash within many of these states, the ability of Josephus to straddle Rome and Jerusalem came to seem all the more pertinent. So too did his own assertion 'without feeling any shame' that he had achieved this through his prophecy to precisely the Roman generals who had inflicted on Jews the greatest loss for which they still mourned after nearly two millennia. For Jewish intellectuals who adopted the ideas of the Enlightenment and might wish to celebrate Josephus as a classical author to be ranked with pride as a Jew alongside the celebrated writers of Greek and Roman antiquity, passing a moral judgment on Josephus for his political stance could feel very personal and raise strong passions.

In 1808–9, the Hebrew journal *HaMe'assef*, which had been founded in Germany in 1784 with the support of the philosopher Moses Mendelssohn to bring to Hebrew literature the best qualities of the Enlightenment, described Josephus as 'one of the greatest of the ancient scholars and recorders of history' who had 'fought in the army, and was a pious and God-fearing person'. In England the prolific novelist Grace Aguilar (1816–47) published in 1845 a remarkable series of portraits, titled *Women of Israel*, which she claimed to have based on 'the revered historian' Josephus, who could be trusted as 'our own historian' of the siege of Jerusalem.[2]

But by 1838 Shalom haKohen, another representative of the Hebrew Enlightenment, was expressing disgust in his history book *Korei haDorot*, published in Warsaw, at Josephus's decision to put his personal interests above those of his fellow Jews, and such condemnation was becoming common among Jews across Europe by the 1850s. A certain 'Hertz ben Pinchas', the pseudonym of a prolific contributor to the *Jewish Chronicle* in London from 1846 to 1870s about whom nothing is known except that he wrote from Manchester and that English was not his native language, lamented in 1851, in an essay titled *Post-Biblical Judaism*, the role of Josephus at Jotapata:

> Jotapata fell because, among the myriads of Jewish warriors, there was one traitor, who preferred an ignominious life to a glorious death. . . . A pang of bitter maddening disappointment pierces the heart, to think that Josephus, the very man who contributed so much to this glorious defence, should himself have been the only warrior who surrendered to the Romans, and thus entailed a suspicion on his name which must for ever cling to his memory.

In the children's section of the *Jewish Chronicle* on 6 January 1911, a boy named Edward expressed similar dismay when he compared Josephus's cowardice to the heroism of Judas Maccabee in a letter sent to 'Auntie' to thank her for the prize of 'the works of Josephus', which she had sent him for the missing-letter competition:

> I have long been anxious to know the sad history of the wars between our nation and the Romans. Now I shall have the opportunity of learning it from Flavius Josephus [here the name 'Yosef ben Mattatiyahu' is inserted in heavy Hebrew type] himself the leader and historian of the same war, but I am disappointed in his behavior in deserting his people by going over to their enemies the Romans. I, myself, would not desert my people in their need. I would stay with them till my last drop of blood lasted, as Judas Maccabaeus did, whose name we remember with great glory and honor, especially on this festival of Chanucah. Best regards to all cousins. I am your sincere nephew, E. Baron.

'Auntie' replied diplomatically that 'the example of Judas Maccabaeus is indeed one for all of us to follow', ignoring the criticism of Josephus.[3]

The problem for 'Auntie' was that by no means would all her readers have agreed with the condemnation of Josephus the man. The first modern biography of Josephus, which had appeared in two parts in the periodical *Jüdisch-deutsche Monatsschrift* and was published in Prague in February and July 1802, was in fact highly favorable. The brief biography, written in standard German but printed in Hebrew letters, was composed by a certain Dr. Lessing (about whom nothing more is known). Josephus's career is presented with romantic color, following closely the narrative of Josephus's autobiography in the *Life* but assigning to its hero not only righteousness, diligence, discipline, and moderation but also common sense in rejecting opposition to Rome and national fervor in serving his people when called upon to do so. Josephus's great reputation as author of superb works of history to establish his own fame and that of his people came only after he had been arrested by Roman forces.

Similarly positive views had been expressed in the Hebrew periodical *HaMe'assef* in Germany twenty years earlier in 1787–88, when Josephus was described as 'a pious and God-fearing person' whose ability to combine these personal qualities with fighting in the army made him close to the ideal 'New Jew' envisaged by the members of the Hebrew Enlightenment. Indeed, over the nineteenth century the identification of many of these 'enlightened' Jews (*maskilim*) with Josephus was sufficient for Moshe Leib Lilienblum, a former *maskil* who threw himself after 1880 into the nationalist movement that was to emerge as Zionism, to blame in 1885 Jews like the *maskilim* themselves for the failure of revolt against Rome: 'only the *assimilated maskilim*, those that loved the Romans and were proficient in Greek literature, like Josephus Flavius, were responsible for the destruction'.[4]

Enthusiasm for Josephus as a Jewish hero can be seen on a curious plaque erected in the Temple Buffault in Paris in 1877 at the instigation of the eccentric philanthropist Daniel Iffla (1825–1907), who adopted the name Daniel Osiris and, despite his first marriage to a Christian woman, funded the building of many synagogues, including this monumental edifice for the use of French Jews following the Portuguese rite.

From a Moroccan family, Osiris amassed an enormous fortune from banking, much of which he spent on a wide

FIGURE 4.1 Josephus listed as 'illustrious child of Israel' on a plaque in Temple Buffault, Paris, erected 1877. Photo, courtesy of Synagogue Buffault.

variety of charitable causes, presenting himself as a great French patriot and leaving his fortune eventually to the Pasteur Institute. He was frequently in conflict with the Consistoire Israélite, which had been established by Napoleon to administer Jewish worship in France, and it is highly unlikely that his idiosyncratic selection of heroes of the Jewish past will have been shared by all, or indeed many, other French Jews. Underneath the headings 'Gloire à Dieu' and 'Aux illustres enfants d' Israel' are portrayed two schematic tablets of the Law, with nineteen names on the left and seventeen on the right. 'Josèphe FLAVIUS' is the eleventh name on the left, after Moses, Samuel, David, Isaiah, Ezra, Hillel, Yohanan ben Zakkai, Akiba, Philo, and 'Juda le Saint'. He is followed by Saadia Gaon and Rashi. The names on the right begin with Moses Mendelsohn and two composers, Meyerbeer and Fromental Halevy. It may well be that the attraction of Josephus for Osiris, like that of some of the other 'heroes', lay precisely in his ability to claim prominence both in the Jewish and in the wider gentile world, as Osiris himself wished to do.[5]

These varying Jewish evaluations of Josephus as a man go back to disputes among the most influential Jewish historians in Germany and France in the first half of the nineteenth century. Isaak Markus Jost (1793–1860), an older contemporary of Eberhard Reuss and one of the first Jews to benefit both from a traditional Jewish education (including Talmud) and from a university education in Germany, became the 'father of modern Jewish historiography'. He used Josephus heavily as his main source for his history of the late Second Temple period, published in the early 1820s. He treated Josephus rather gently, mentioning (for instance) only briefly his change of sides at Jotapata. He was unsympathetic to what he saw as vainglorious self-justification in the *Life*, but he distinguished specifically between Josephus as a Jew and a priest and Josephus as a politician and general, and he distinguished both from Josephus the writer. Jost, like Reuss, had known the turmoil of the Napoleonic Wars and could identify with Josephus as a man who had survived such a period of turmoil and subsequently tried to blend in to the victorious regime without denying his identity as a Jew. Indeed, Jost identified himself with Josephus so much that he was ranked with Josephus in the oration delivered at his funeral in 1860, when his friend Leopold Stein described Jost and Josephus as the only true Jewish historians.[6]

Joseph Salvador (1796–1873) was only three years younger than Jost but hailed from a very different milieu. Born in Montpellier in the south of France, Salvador was the offspring of a Sephardic father and Catholic mother. He was more concerned to stress the importance of the Jewish legacy for the Saint-Simonian movement in contemporary France than to trace Jewish history soberly through the evidence as Jost tried to do. He had little sympathy for Josephus. In his *Histoire de la Domination Romaine en Judée et de la Ruine de Jerusalem* (1847), he portrayed Josephus as a willing representative of the privileged oppressors of the people who had crushed Jerusalem under siege. For Salvador, Josephus's frequent claims that thieves and robbers were to blame for the ruin of the city were evidence that he was a self-interested collaborator. The discrepancies between the account of the Galilee campaign in the *Jewish War* and the *Life* showed not just a faulty memory (as for

Jost) but the disjunction between Josephus's public face as rebel leader and his private role as Roman stooge.[7]

The enthusiastic reception by many Jews of Salvador's attack on Josephus owed much to timing, with the outbreak of revolutions across Europe in 1846–48 followed all too rapidly by their suppression. The villain described by Salvador was easier to recognize than the more complex figure depicted by Jost. The obliteration of liberal hopes in 1848 reverberated through historiography of all kinds, including among Jews—and not least the most influential Jewish historian of the nineteenth century, Heinrich Graetz.

Graetz was in his early thirties in 1848. For a democrat longing for the full emancipation of the Jews, which was set back in much of Europe by the failure of liberalism in 1848, the compromised figure of Josephus was inevitably ambiguous, but in many respects he saw himself as a champion of enlightened orthodoxy during the emergence of Reform Judaism in Germany. As a historian with a particular interest in the end of the Second Temple period, he had little choice but to rely on Josephus. Graetz chose to publish the volumes of his great history not in chronological order but as they were completed. Thus volume 4 of his *History*, on the years after 70 CE, was the first volume to be published, in 1853. It was closely followed in 1856 by volume 3, which covered the period from the mid-second century BCE to the destruction of Jerusalem. Both volumes used Josephus as a primary source. But Graetz, swept along by the judgment of Salvador (and also Reuss, whose *Encyclopedie* article had been published the previous year), was driven to query how a *Römling* like Josephus was selected to be general of Galilee in the first place.

Much of the agonizing over Josephus's political stance derived from the discrepant account of the Galilee campaign in the *Life* compared to the *Jewish War* and the impossibility of straightforward reconciliation of the two: either Josephus threw himself wholeheartedly into his role as rebel commander (as in the *Jewish War*) or he was from the start seeking rapprochement with Rome (as in the *Life*). Theories put forward in the 1850s and 1860s became more and more complex, often relying (implausibly) on the notion that the two accounts were written for wholly different readerships. By 1878, when the third edition of volume 3 of Graetz's *History* was published, a new footnote tried to get the best of all worlds by claiming that Josephus, who had been 'moderate' in 66 CE, was caught up in the passion of the revolt to which he dedicated himself sincerely, only to suffer gradual disillusionment in the following months and eventually to make a secret compact with the Romans. In the Germany of Bismarck, Graetz would not wish to suggest that Josephus should obviously have opposed the Roman state in case he might seem to imply that German Jews should question their loyalty to the new German state.[8]

Graetz was not alone in his dilemma in the 1870s. Josephus's political stance during the war was widely debated, not always with great subtlety but with particular sophistication in Breslau, where Graetz had taught for many years in the Jewish Theological Seminary and held the title of honorary professor since 1869. An invitation to a meeting on a Sunday morning to hear a yearly report on religious classes for children in Breslau in 1873 included a learned article by J. Prager, a student of Graetz, on the relation of Flavius

Josephus to the Zealots at the outbreak of the war; whether all who were sent the invitation fully appreciated the nuances of the argument or checked the impressive array of references in the forty-eight footnotes may be doubted, but it is significant that the organizers of the meeting considered the topic appropriate for a serious institution such as theirs. Also in Breslau, in 1877, Aron Baerwald submitted a whole dissertation devoted to analysis of the political career of Josephus in Galilee, evolving a complicated theory of conspiracy between Josephus and Agrippa II. Two decades later, Josephus's political career was being earnestly discussed in Russia by Simon Dubnow in his *Textbook on Jewish History for Jewish Youth*, published in 1898–99. Dubnow himself was markedly sympathetic to Josephus's dilemma. A dedicated activist who devoted himself to promoting Jewish civil rights in Russia, rejecting both assimilation and Zionism, Dubnow developed the view that Josephus had aligned himself with Rome not out of treachery but in rational recognition of the superiority of Roman government and secular knowledge to that of Jews in his day.[9]

In England, the debate can be traced through the pages of the *Jewish Chronicle*, where in 1855 the editor had remarked that 'the writings of both Moses and Josephus are in the hands of everyone'—presumably in the Whiston translation, which was much the most commonly available and indeed sold by the newspaper up to 1852–53, when sales stopped, perhaps out of concern for the inadequacies of the translation, which were often noted. Fascination with Josephus was not continuous, and a correspondent to the *Chronicle* complained in 1907 that his works were less well known in his day than they had been two generations earlier, but references to his writings are common in the first third of the twentieth century, with the battle lines on his politics clearly delineated: in 1915, during the Great War, Herbert Loewe, who had recently been appointed to a post as lecturer in Oriental languages in Exeter College in Oxford but was then in India engaged in war work, protested Josephus's heroism against the skepticism expressed by the Zionist Norman Bentwich in a book on Josephus published the year previously. In 1921 the learned Dr. Abraham Cohen of the Birmingham Hebrew Congregation sought to have the best of all worlds by describing Josephus as a great historian despite having been a traitor, renegade, and sycophant.[10]

But the moral issues raised by Josephus's political choices were evidently most stark during the turmoil for Jews in Europe and the Middle East in the 1930s and 1940s. In Antwerp a mock trial of Josephus by some Jewish law students in 1937 found him guilty of treason. A schoolboy in the Vilna ghetto recorded in his diary on 7 March 1943 his participation in a similar trial of Josephus; Josephus's role in standing between Rome and the rebels was all too pertinent as the Judenrat was attempting to protect the inhabitants of the ghetto from Nazi oppression. In France, a trial held by members of the French Resistance unequivocally condemned Josephus for his collaboration. Such mock trials became staple fare among Zionist youth groups such as Bnei Akiva in Palestine in the 1940s and 1950s. The political scientist Shlomo Avineri wrote in 2010 in *Haaretz* about a trial held in 1948 in his youth group, in which Yohanan ben Zakkai was accused alongside Josephus for having abandoned Jerusalem during the Roman siege, and both defendants were acquitted on the basis of their later contributions to the Jewish people. His younger contemporary at the Hebrew University, Avishai Margalit, recalled in 2012 being 'condemned' as Josephus sixty years previously, at the age of thirteen, when he attempted to defend Josephus's actions by comparing him to Jeremiah. Condemnation was normal, although a trial broadcast on Israeli television in 1992 ended with Josephus's acquittal for lack of evidence. The ambiguity continues in decisions about street names in Israel: in the 1920s a joint committee of Jews and Arabs under the chairmanship of Sir Ronald Storrs, civil governor of Jerusalem under the British Mandate, gave a road in the city the name 'Josephus Street', but after 1948 this was changed to its current name, 'Yosef ben Mattitiyahu Street'. The new name commemorates the revolutionary general and does not refer to Josephus as a writer; by contrast, 'Flavius Josephus Street' in Beersheva is located in a district commemorating Jewish historians.[11]

The Book among Christians

Even as debate raged among Jews about the morality and political judgment of the author of the *Jewish War*, the book itself received attention throughout the nineteenth and twentieth centuries to a greater degree than at any time since its composition, becoming the best known of Josephus's works and with a wide and varied readership in vernacular translations, particularly in the English-speaking world.

At the beginning of the nineteenth century a Catholic theologian from the University of Würzburg introduced Johann Bernhard Frise's new translation of the *Jewish War* into

German, published in Altona in two volumes in 1804–5, with 116 pages about the *Testimonium Flavianum*, even though the purported reference to Jesus was to be found in the *Antiquities* and not in the *Jewish War*. The theologian, Franz Oberthür, noted sarcastically that when he was engaged in social conversation and his expertise in studies of Josephus became known, 'practically the only question' put to him was his opinion of 'Josephus's well-known testimony of Christ . . . as if nothing else was contained in the writings of this Jewish writer . . . or as though this passage was the most significant of the significant passages of Josephus's writings'. Oberthür himself was dubious about the genuineness of the *Testimonium*, but his long 'Vorrede' did nothing to undermine the centrality of such specifically Christian concerns for German readers of Josephus through the rest of the nineteenth century. In 1852, Konrad Martin, professor of theology in Bonn, announced in the introduction to his new translation of Josephus's *Jewish Antiquities* that he wished to return the book to the homes of Christian families 'as a type of house or family book'.[12]

In English a new translation of the *Jewish War* by Robert Traill was published posthumously in 1851 after Traill, a Calvinist clergyman in County Cork, died of typhus in 1847 following valiant efforts to bring some relief to the needy during the great famine in Ireland. Traill's version challenged both the quality and the theological reliability of Whiston's translation of 1737, but the preeminence of Whiston both in England and in North America was too firmly established to be shaken, and it was Whiston's version of Josephus's works that was translated into Welsh in Dolgellau in 1819 and in Caernarfon in 1860. The precise

FIGURE 4.2 Josephus as Oriental, engraving after a drawing by Lizars. Portrait facing the title page of an edition of the English translation of Josephus's works by William Whiston (Edinburgh, 1865).

number of reprints of Whiston is hard to establish, since they were produced at many different presses in England, Scotland, Ireland, and the United States and often lack any information on the publisher. A notable characteristic of some of them is the addition of a long and detailed account of the more recent history of the Jews, with a focus on the rights accorded to Jews in recent decades in England, composed by an anonymous author or authors.

Such additions to the original history are eloquent testimony to the prestige not just of Josephus but, more specifically, of the Whiston translation, often much enhanced by impressive binding and numerous illustrations. They are testimony also to a view of Josephus as more than just a prop to a Christian agenda. The ambivalent attitude to Jews found in these anonymous sequels to Whiston's text would fit well with a Christian Zionist model that Jews as a nation continued to play a central role in the unfolding of God's plans for humanity such as were espoused by Lord Shaftesbury, who published in 1841 a 'Memorandum to Protestant Monarchs of Europe for the Restoration of the Jews to Palestine' in the belief that the gathering of the Jews in Israel would bring about the Second Coming of Christ. Most such Christian Zionists affirmed that in the final days the Jews would all be converted to Christianity. But in some later versions of American Christian Zionism, under the influence of John Nelson Derby, a nineteenth-century Anglo-Irish clergyman who helped to form the movements now known as the Plymouth Brethren and the Exclusive Brethren, the eventual fate of the Jews was to be annihilated.

The Whiston edition is what the novelist will have expected his readers to have in mind when Thomas Hardy referred in passing in 1886 to the folio of Josephus on the dining room table of the mayor of Casterbridge. The 'book called "Josephus", an old leather-bound volume, smelling of a hundred voyages, very solid and very like the Bible, but enlivened with accounts of battles and sieges', which Rudyard

Kipling portrayed as suitable Sunday reading for American fishermen in *Captains Courageous*, published in 1897, would have been a copy of Whiston. And it would have been the *Jewish War* in Whiston's translation to which Mark Twain alluded in 1872 in his semiautobiographical humorous memoir of his travels with his brother in the Wild West, when he notes in cheerful fashion that 'I felt rowdyish and "bully", (as the historian Josephus phrases it, in his fine chapter upon the destruction of the Temple)'. A contemporary of Mark Twain in America, General Lew Wallace, reported in his autobiography that in 1873 at the Library of Congress, where he researched 'everything on the shelves relating to the Jews', he found in Whiston's Josephus the raw material for his immensely popular novel *Ben-Hur: A Tale of the Christ* (1880), which was to inspire, not least through a Broadway production and films (including the 1959 epic), a whole industry in the United States in the twentieth century. The basis of this fascination was a concern to imagine the origins of Christianity, as the title of the novel suggests, but the main effect was a fashion for the excesses of imperial Rome as depicted in set-piece scenes such as the chariot race in the film of 1959.[13]

As universities established clearer borders for academic disciplines both in Europe and in the Americas, the study of Josephus was not fully embraced within academic classical studies until the twentieth century. Josephus's writings were not prized for their literary qualities, and in the nineteenth century classicists mostly confined themselves to the task of editing the Greek text. Thus the definitive edition of Josephus's writings was the work of Benedict Niese, son of a pastor, who was professor of classical philology at the University of Marburg from 1885 when his edition was being printed in Berlin (between 1885 and 1895). Niese would move (in 1906, at the age of fifty-seven) to a post as professor of ancient history at Halle, but he evinced no interest in using Josephus for ancient history. The same was true of Niese's older contemporary Samuel Adrianus Naber, who was a professor of Greek and Latin at the University of Amsterdam from 1871 to 1989. Naber's rival edition of Josephus's works, published by Teubner in Leipzig in 1888–96, followed the school of the Dutch scholar Carel Gabriel Cobet in assuming the right, and indeed the duty, of the editor to subject the text as received in the manuscripts to extensive emendations to make it accord with his own understanding of good Greek and the probable intention of the author, but his edition never challenged the authority of Niese's. In France, the project directed in the first decades of the twentieth century by the wealthy Jewish polymath Theodore Reinach, to produce a new and more accurate French translation of Josephus's works, was undertaken under the auspices of the Societé des Etudes Juives, in the spirit of the Wissenschaft des Judenthums, rather than the wider world of classical studies within which Reinach occupied a prominent position.

As a historian concerned to understand the world of the New Testament, the German Protestant theologian Emil Schürer did not hesitate to use Josephus's works as a primary source of his *Lehrbuch der neutestamentlichen Zeitgeschichte* (1874), but historians of the Roman world paid little attention to the *Jewish War*. Wilhelm Weber, who taught ancient history in a number of major German universities during and after the First World War and became a fervent admirer of Adolf Hitler, devoted his *Josephus und Vespasian*, published in Stuttgart in 1921, to a discussion of the non-Jewish sources used by Josephus as the base of his narrative. Within the English-speaking world, much of the most important work on the text of Josephus's writings and the use of the *Jewish War* for history was carried out by the English biblical scholar Henry St. John Thackeray (1869–1930), who specialized in *koine* rather than classical Greek and spent much effort on the study of Saint Paul and of the Septuagint when not devoted to Josephus. Thackeray, who had been a scholar in Cambridge in the last decade of the nineteenth century, had a huge influence on understanding of the *Jewish War* both through the Hilda Stroock Lectures delivered in 1927 in New York, published in 1929 as *Josephus: The Man and the Historian*, and as editor and translator of Josephus's works for the widely disseminated bilingual edition in the Loeb Classical Library series published by Harvard University Press. It is sobering to note that Thackeray's prodigious scholarly output was achieved in the leisure time afforded to him from his main employment as a civil servant.

It would be great to imagine that scholarship as fine as Thackeray's would have had a decisive influence on the life of the *Jewish War*, but this has not been the case for all English readers. Thackeray's translation was much used by Geoffrey Williamson, a classics teacher at Norwich School whose version of the *Jewish War*, first published by Penguin in 1959, has been widely used on both sides of the Atlantic, and it has also exercised some influence on the new translation by Martin Hammond published in Oxford in 2017, but the English text still most commonly cited—in part because it is freely available on the internet—remains, disconcertingly, the work of Whiston.

The Book among Jews

Among Jews in nineteenth-century Germany, the *Jewish War* provided one of the best of all possible sources for establishing the right of Jews to be considered a people like others whose origins could be traced back to classical antiquity. For the Wissenschaft des Judentums ('Science of Judaism') movement, which sought to construct a national history based on a land, political institutions, military achievements, and cultural distinctiveness, the writings of Josephus, and, above all, the *Jewish War*, provided precious evidence that Jews could be studied with the same critical tools as the ancient Greeks and Romans. If the traditions about the Jewish past preserved in the rabbinic tradition could somehow be brought into line with the clear political narrative of Josephus's history, the Jews would come to be seen not just as a people like any other but as a nation with a history of exceptional glory and pathos. If Josephus told the story of Jewish rebellion against Rome, that should be celebrated alongside the heroic nationalist opposition to Rome by Arminius in Germany, Vercingetorix in Gaul, and Boudicca in Britain.

Bringing the *Jewish War* into the orbit of classical philology, and therefore presenting Josephus's history as equivalent to the works of the Greek and Latin historians viewed by educated Europeans as the bedrock of their culture, was not straightforward. As we have seen, classical philologists in the first half of the nineteenth century stuck generally to the immediate context of Athens and Rome and avoided contamination from the Semitic world, including the Greek literature of the Jews. But Jewish scholars, keen to break away from a history composed solely of religious teachings, were less hesitant.

The origins of the Wissenschaft des Judentums lay in fact in a radical new approach to the story not of Jewish literature in Greek but of the rabbinic tradition that had been the main focus of Jewish education for so many centuries. It began with the publication in 1818 of an article by Leopold Zunz titled 'Etwas über die rabbinische Literatur' ('Something on rabbinical literature'), which set out an academic approach to ancient Jewish texts that would take account of historical context and cross-cultural comparisons. Zunz himself never really tackled Josephus, devoting his subsequent career to studies of liturgy and biblical exegesis, but the *Verein für Kultur und Wissenschaft der Juden*, which he founded in Berlin in 1819, and the *Zeitschrift für die Wissenschaft des Judentums*, which he edited in 1823, placed the writing of Jewish history at the center of the new 'science'.

Hence the use of the *Jewish War* by Jost, the 'father of modern Jewish historiography', who had been one of Zunz's collaborators in the foundation of the *Verein*. It is characteristic of the self-conscious alignment of these Jewish scholars with the new standards of philology that Josephus's writings were used only with a dose of criticism about the inadequacy of the Haverkamp edition of 1726 on which Jost felt forced to rely in the first volume of his *Geschichte*, published in Berlin in 1820. But this did not prevent him from using the *Jewish War* for the second volume in 1821, which dealt with the Roman war itself, even accepting Josephus's assertion that Titus had been innocent of any plan to destroy the Temple. Jost reckoned that the immediacy of the *Jewish War*, written so soon after the conflict it described, provided grounds to accept its testimony in preference to differing versions in Josephus's later writings, which (in his view) suffered from failing memory and too much Hellenistic rhetoric. On the other hand he showed himself well aware, in a discussion in an appendix of 'the historian Josephus as such', that the brevity of Josephus's political career in Galilee might explain the shortcomings of his account of military affairs. He also noted that Josephus's circumstances after 70 were bound to have affected the way he described the war: 'Josephus wrote in Rome, as a prisoner. The more his representations complied with the spirit and the views of the Romans, the better his fate. A non-Jew and a free man probably would have seen the events differently'.[14]

We have seen that Jost's high estimation of the value of the *Jewish War* as a historical source was shared by the most influential historian to emerge from the Wissenschaft des Judentums movement, despite Graetz's eventual disparagement of Josephus as a 'Römling'. For Graetz, Josephus's testimony to the misery of Jews under Herod, when rebellious youths were prepared to accept death when caught trying to pull down the image of an eagle that Herod had set up above the Temple (1.653), provided the Sitz in Leben of the composition of the biblical book of Ecclesiastes, which declared that 'the day of death is better than the day of one's birth' (Eccl. 7:1). Graetz was quite prepared to use any evidence he could find in the *Jewish War* regardless of inconsistencies. In some respects, his approach marked a retreat from the critical and nuanced, but dry, scholarship of Jost three decades earlier. The lofty intellectual aims of the original Wissenschaft movement were all too easily co-opted into writing about the past as a way to engineer change in the present.

Leopold Zunz noted in a letter his approval of a plan by Philip Ehrenberg to write an account of the destruction of Jerusalem to counter Jost's careful history, 'to honour the rights of the patriotic Zealots, and to put the far too highly estimated Titus a bit more into the right light'. Zunz agreed with Ehrenberg that 'a narration of the Vespasian War has not been undertaken from a Jewish national point of view', and that this could be done only by using the *Jewish War* as a source for the narrative but ignoring Josephus's views: 'We must not forget that we hear in his [Josephus's] account only one party: the peace party'. The letter was written in February 1847, in the febrile atmosphere leading up to the revolutions of 1848 by which Zunz himself set great store.[15]

The impulse to objective scholarship relying on a variety of sources, critical analysis, and philology that underlay the Wissenschaft movement arose to a considerable extent in opposition to the constraints of traditional religious orthodoxy. Many (though not all) of the original founders of the movement identified in one way or another with Reform within German Judaism. But just as Zunz could co-opt history to advance his ideology of emancipation and acculturation, so too could orthodox historians co-opt Josephus for the composition of Jewish history designed to enhance commitment to the rabbinic tradition as it had developed over the generations.

The impact of the techniques of Wissenschaft scholarship on the orthodox world by the mid-nineteenth century can be gauged from the proliferation in Eastern Europe of traditional chronicles of the lives of rabbinic sages with the addition of a scholarly, or pseudo-scholarly, apparatus. Such biographies have been described by Ada

Rappaport-Albert as 'hagiography with footnotes', but Isaac Halevy, whose *Dorot haRishonim* ('First Generations') was published in a series of volumes from 1897, was much more serious in his approach.

Halevy, born in Lithuania and educated in the prestigious Lithuanian yeshiva in Volozhin (now Valozhyn in Belarus), was forced into a life of wandering in his late forties when his business went bankrupt in 1895, and his historical writings, produced while he was in Germany, represent an attempt to bring together the orthodox worlds of Eastern and Central Europe. For Halevy, both faith and historical scholarship sought the truth, and the science of history provides the orthodox Jew with the means to anchor his faith. It was in this spirit that Halevy approached the use of the *Jewish War* as a source, with techniques surprisingly close to those in standard use in modern critical scholarship.[16]

For Halevy it was self-evident that Josephus was a flawed witness to the events he described, 'so accustomed to guile and intrigue that he became inured to them and wrote these things without sensing that they would have been better left unwritten'. He accused Josephus of treason, not least in allowing Galilee to fall so easily into the hands of Vespasian, and for encouraging anti-Semitism in his writings by blaming the Jews for the revolt: 'No wonder that ever since then the Romans looked upon the Jews with contempt as upon an inferior people, and we experience this ourselves to this very day'. Josephus 'writes with unconcealed contempt for Torah scholars, speaking out against them openly as against implacable enemies', and he supports the enemies of the Jewish nation: 'The welcome extended to Josephus by Titus and Vespasian upon his emergence from the cave indicates that they did not view him as adversary and subversive to their aims, rather as one who aided and abetted their task'.

Some of these accusations would have been very hard to sustain from anything that Josephus actually wrote, since (for instance) he never referred to Torah scholars, but it is all the more striking that Halevy used these polemical judgments as cover for basing much of his history on Josephus's testimony, on the grounds that sometimes 'Josephus's words are not a mere expression which can be dismissed as inaccurate, nor mere rhetorical flourishes which may be ignored; rather, these are accounts of actual events expressed directly and consistent with what he writes elsewhere'. Halevy proposed a clear method for using Josephus as a source: once Josephus's agenda has been discerned, the student can assume that details that are not compatible with this agenda were incorporated into his narrative only because they reflected what really happened. The technique allows the modern scholar to rely on Josephus's description of specific events while remaining skeptical about his overall narrative, putting the nuggets of truth that emerge from Josephus's writings into a balanced reconstruction, since, as Halevy noted, 'we have noticed frequently that Josephus has one great quality: that however he may have tried to mislead his readers and mask his face with his cloak, there are kernels of truth scattered amongst his writings here and there. We must merely gather them together from different points and they will indicate to us reliable views'. Such techniques allowed Halevy occasionally not only to extract information from the *Jewish War* but also to celebrate openly the value of his testimony in contrast to rabbinic traditions, noting 'how amazing it is to hear such things in the marketplace of life, not from the walls of the house of study or the tents of Torah, but from the word of Josephus Flavius, who was dwelling at that time in the halls of Vespasian and Titus'. Like all good scholars, he feels reassured when Josephus's account is confirmed by other sources, whether rabbinic or non-Jewish, but he is unequivocal that Josephus's works need to be taken into account when they constitute, as they often do, 'the single source for all the chronicles of those times'. Halevy's efforts helped to establish the writings of Josephus as an acceptable historical source within orthodox circles, albeit not necessarily for what he may have considered the right reasons. Among those who declared that Josephus's works could be used was Israel Meir Kagan, known (after the title of his first book) as the Hafetz Hayyim. The Hafetz Hayyim, who was one of the most influential figures in orthodox Judaism in Eastern Europe in the last half of the nineteenth century and the first decades of the twentieth, was inclined to approve of the use of Josephus on the grounds that he should be identified with Yosippon, who was cited by the medieval rabbinic authorities and could therefore be treated as kosher. When the Hafetz Hayyim was told that this Yosippon was said to have been a Sadducee, he simply indicated that he considered this unlikely.[17]

Halevy's work was impressively independent, but his Hebrew was inelegant and he does not seem to have gained a large readership. By contrast, a larger orthodox audience was attracted to the religious Zionist history composed by his contemporary Ze'ev Yavetz, whose *Toledot Yisrael* ('History of Israel') was published in a series of volumes from 1895. Yavetz, from northeast Poland, migrated for a period to Palestine but moved back north to Vilna in 1897 and lived in later years in Germany, Antwerp, and, eventually, England. Committed to demonstrating the national bond that held the Jews together and 'the power and value of halakhah and its role in the history of the people of Israel', Yavetz was nonetheless open to the use of non-Jewish sources, such as Cassius Dio and Eusebius, and saw himself as committed to an objective scholarly approach, albeit on the assumption that it is essential 'to critique the conduct of Israel in the spirit of Israel and from within its own literature'. It was in this spirit that he approached the *Jewish War* as a historical source.[18]

Both Yavetz and Halevy had established reputations as scientific historians within the orthodox world by the early 1900s. Halevy considered Yavetz to be insufficiently rigorous in his approach and took him to task for weaving biographies of rabbinic sages into his writings, but both writers were agreed in considering Josephus to have been a wicked traitor and Roman collaborator whose writings nonetheless provide essential insights into the history of the Jewish people. Yavetz went to town in his description of Josephus's failed campaign in Galilee, in the course of which, he asserted, Josephus 'pillaged, in his impetuous and capricious villainy, the northern battlements protecting Jerusalem from the Roman persecutor'. But none of this vituperation prevented him from referring to Josephus's testimony hundreds of times in his *History*, and when he came to provide a considered account of Josephus's writings, in volume 6 of the *History*, which deals with the period after 70 CE, he was almost sympathetic in some of his comments: Josephus might have been surprised to receive approbation for his open expression of distress at the calamities that had befallen his nation, since he had confessed specifically that such personal interjections were inappropriate in a history (1.12), but Yavetz evidently believed such commitment to be praiseworthy. In the end, Yavetz, like Halevy, was in no doubt about the value of Josephus's writings for orthodox Jews in his time: 'Thousands of years have passed over the works of Josephus, with hardly a person of Israel having read them, and the reticence shown towards them by all the Sages of the diaspora has been to the great detriment of the historiography of Israel. . . . Since the scholars of Israel have begun to return to study these works, the times of the Second Temple period are much more clearly understood'.[19]

Yavetz cited the *Jewish War* not independently but through the Hebrew translation, published by Kalman Schulman in 1862, which had a huge impact in bringing Josephus's history into the world of enlightened Hebrew readers among the Jewish population of Eastern and Central Europe. Kalman Schulman, born into a Hasidic family in Russia in 1819, studied in the Volozhin yeshiva and in his middle age became a leading figure among the Jews of Vilna in the burgeoning Haskalah movement, which aimed to regenerate Jewish society specifically by providing Jews with books in Hebrew on science, philosophy, geography, history, poetry, and (by the 1850s) fiction. Within these circles, Schulman had done well for himself by publishing a Hebrew translation of the novel *Mysteries of Paris* by Eugène Sue, but the enterprise had also engendered criticism from other *maskilim*, who felt that bringing gentile fiction to Jews was not their mission, and Schulman responded with a project to translate all the works of Josephus, restoring to the Jews the works of an ancient Jewish writer that had been dressed in 'foreign garments' heretofore: 'I should honestly say that no-one before me did such a great thing in the field of Hebrew literature'.[20]

The Josephus project seems to have been given considerable support from the start by the Vilna *maskilim*. The new Hebrew periodical *HaKarmel* published in 1861 an open letter by Schulman soliciting advanced subscribers, with an assertion that it was high time to put into Hebrew the work of 'the noblest of all the writers of antiquities in their generations and the first of all of authors of ancient history'. Josephus was described as 'the anointed priest' and his works as 'wonderful'. The timing was clearly opportune—indeed, so opportune that it emerged that another Hebrew translation of Josephus's *Life* was under way. For a while it looked as if there might be competition, but the other translation never appeared. When the *Jewish War* appeared in two parts in 1861–62, published by Romm, it was acclaimed.

Schulman claimed for his translation that he wrote in 'clear and dynamic Hebrew' and that his book would be distinguished by its scholarly tone, with notes and annotations, but in fact its success lay to a great degree in its dramatic force and its uncompromising acceptance of Josephus on his own terms, saving Josephus 'from the defamation he has suffered from members of our people, the scholars of Germany'. For Schulman, Josephus was a hero and model like the prophet Jeremiah, and the criticisms of contemporary German historians, particularly Graetz, were simply misguided.[21]

Despite his claims to scholarly rigor, Schulman made use not of Josephus's original Greek text as the basis of his translation but of the German version published by the New Testament scholar Heinrich Paret in 1855 as *Geschichte des Jüdischen Krieges*. There was nothing unusual among *maskilic* translators in translating from the German, but what was unusual was Schulman's failure to mention Paret in his publication. It seems that, whereas for many works reference to the latest German edition was proof of serious scholarly credentials, in the case of a Jewish author being reclaimed for his nation it was better for the translator to give the impression that he had gone back to the original, even if this was not in fact true. And in practice Schulman made huge changes to his source text. Paret had stayed close to the Greek, simply adding clarificatory footnotes on historical issues for the benefit of students of first-century Judaea, and Schulman ensured a scholarly patina for his own version by retaining Paret's full text without omissions and maintaining Paret's divisions into books, chapters, and sections, but the translation itself was greatly adapted to make Josephus's words sound at home in the Hebrew language.[22]

This process was helped, of course, by the preference of *maskilim* in Russia for biblical Hebrew as their translation language and the appropriateness of a biblical mode to express the subject matter of the *Jewish War*. The process of making that text sound familiarly Jewish to general Jewish readers in Eastern Europe involved such techniques as changing the name of 'Matthias, der Sohn des Asamonaios' at *Jewish War* 1.36 to 'Mattatiyahu the Hasmonaean', adding 'king' to the reference to David's grave at 1.61, altering 'Philadelphia' at 1.60 to 'Rabbah of the Ammonites', and referring to 'the Temple of the Lord' where Josephus's original (and Paret) had only 'Temple' (1.32). Such changes, each minor in itself, combine to give a sense of the *Jewish War* as a quintessentially Jewish text, as did the insertion of fragments of biblical verses at moments of heightened description, a practice common in Hebrew novels in this period. So, for instance, Josephus's reference in book 7 to the magnificence and renown of Jerusalem when lamenting its destruction through the madness of the rebels (7.4) was presented with the addition of appropriate phrases from Lamentations (1:1; 2:15): 'Is this the city of which they say she is great among the nations, a princess among the provinces, perfection of beauty and the joy of all the lands of the east?' Schulman's choice to give the title of the book in the plural (as *The Wars of the Jews*) was not derived from Paret, who named the book *Geschichte des Juedischen Krieges*, but it was in line with the work of some earlier translators into other languages, although it is unlikely that he was influenced by them. Whatever the reason for his decision, the plural in the title may have helped traditional Jews to align Josephus's narrative with the standard Talmudic explanation for the fall of the Second Temple as divine retribution for unwarranted strife between Jewish factions in Jerusalem.[23]

The exceptional success of Schulman's translation owed much to its readability, like a novel, but it was aided by the reputation of Schulman himself as a man who stood out from other *maskilim* in Vilna for his devotion to religion. His main occupation was as a schoolteacher preparing students for entry into the rabbinical seminary in Vilna which, at the behest of the government of Nicholas I, required a general education in addition to Jewish education in the spirit of the Haskalah. Such education was widely seen as a threat to traditional Jewish values, but unlike other *maskilim*, Schulman avoided any clash with the religious authorities, preferring to present himself as 'a true orthodox in his spirit and behaviour . . . in his side locks that grew below his ears, his long beard and his clothing'. His translation project was explicitly approved by Rabbi Abraham Simhah of the Mastislav community, on the grounds that Schulman was fulfilling the desire of the Gaon of Vilna to have books of science translated into Hebrew. This wish, according to Rabbi Simhah, had been transmitted from the Gaon through Baruch of Shklov to Haim of Volozhin and specifically included the translation of Josephus into Hebrew, 'for through it, we will arrive at an understanding of the intention of our sages of blessed memory in the Talmud and the midrashim'.[24]

The new translation was hailed on its publication by a writer in the Hebrew weekly newspaper *HaMaggid*, published in Lyck in East Prussia (now northeastern Poland): 'For more than eight hundred years Israel did not attain to see the work of Ben Mattityah embellished in Hebrew—until the eloquent and articulate Mr Schulman arose and our desire was fulfilled'. The enthusiasm was testimony not only to Schulman but also to what was by now a long tradition of interest in the translation of Josephus's Greek works into Hebrew among *maskilim*. Salomon Loewisohn published in 1818 in the journal *Sulamith*, one of the main disseminators of the ideas of the early Haskalah, an enthusiastic article (in German) on the parallels between Josephus, Jeremiah, and Isaac Abravanel as witnesses to turning points in Jewish history and as models for coping with disaster. In 1828 Isaac Baer Levinsohn, in his *Te'udah beYisrael*, published in Vilna and Grodno, mentioned that 'Yosef ben Gurion haKohen, one of the notable priests and anointed for war, named Josephus Flavius, wrote his famous books in the

Greek language', providing a brief biography of Josephus in a long footnote. The Galician *maskil* Nachman Krochmal (1785–1840), whose combination of Jewish philosophy with German thought (especially Kant and Hegel) and a critical approach to the study of Jewish history paved the way for the Wissenschaft movement, cited Josephus frequently, quoting at length from his works in his *Moreh Nebukhei haZeman* ('Guide for the Perplexed of the Time'), which was edited posthumously by Leopold Zunz and published in Lemberg in 1851.[25]

Enthusiasm for the *Jewish War* as a foundation document of Jewish national self-consciousness was shared by those Jews who envisaged a Jewish future in the land of Israel as much as by the *maskilim* who sought a national cultural revival in the diaspora, despite the ambivalence of Zionists toward Josephus as a politician who could be deemed to have betrayed his people. Hence the use of Josephus by the Zionist *maskil* Zvi Hirsch Masliansky (1856–1943), who moved from his birth place in Lithuania through Europe in the 1890s to become an immensely influential preacher in New York. Masliansky was capable of drawing large crowds through his oratory in both Yiddish and Hebrew, and his visiting cards proclaimed him '*hamatif hale'umi*' ('the nation's preacher'). He saw himself as a *maskil*, determined to imbibe wider secular culture but within a distinctively Jewish (and religious) environment. He was nearly forty when his dedication to promulgating the ideas of Ahad Ha'am 'for the rebirth of Israel in the Land of Israel' forced him to leave Russia, and he was already well enough known by 1895 for a collection of testimonials to him, as 'the Famous Jewish National Orator', to be published by Joseph Massel, a friend in

Manchester. He evidently found a natural audience in the orthodox East European synagogues in New York in the early 1900s, and a collection of his writings, published in Hebrew in 1929, reveals something of the material from which he constructed his inspiring sermons.[26]

Masliansky took for granted the 'eternal shame' of Josephus as a traitor to his country and betrayer of his people but judged him to have redeemed himself with his writings. Masliansky had met Schulman at his home during his journeys around Jewish communities to spread the word about Zionism and had been much impressed by the old man as a representative of an earlier generation of the Haskalah, so he must have known Schulman's translation of the *Jewish War*, even if his own attitude toward Josephus was markedly less positive. Whether he used the Schulman version directly is uncertain, but there can be no doubt about his interest in Josephus's own career in Galilee as evidence of Josephus's cunning and deceit, in contrast to John of Gischala, who was portrayed as a hero who ended his life in a Roman prison because of his dedication to his people and country. In Masliansky's version of the *Jewish War*, Josephus's account is accepted and embroidered (with, for instance, a claim that Josephus tricked Simon ben Gamaliel, as head of the Sanhedrin, into giving him the command in Galilee), but with Josephus's own judgments about motivation and morality turned on their head.

Masliansky could clearly take for granted that his Jewish audience knew about Josephus and the *Jewish War*, and that the Zionist evaluation of the Jewish rebels as heroes inevitably entailed denigration of Josephus as traitor, but a rather more positive evaluation of both Josephus and his historical writings was being propounded by another Zionist historian in the same decade as the publication of Masliansky's sermons, and on the basis of a much closer acquaintance with the original text written by Josephus. There can be little doubt that appreciation of the significance of Jacob Nafthali Hertz Simchoni as a historian of the Second Temple period would be far greater if he had not died suddenly in Berlin in 1926 at the early age of forty-two before he could take up the position he had been offered to teach Jewish history at the Hebrew University of Jerusalem, which had been officially opened only the previous year. Simchoni (born Simchowitz) came from Slutsk and grew up in an environment dedicated to the Haskalah, studying Latin and Greek as a teenager and gaining a doctorate in Jewish studies in Berlin in 1914. His interests in Jewish history were extensive, but his greatest achievement was his translation of Josephus's writings into Hebrew from the original Greek. His translation of the *Jewish War*, published in Warsaw in 1923, was a work that aimed more seriously than Schulman's to be seen as a work of genuine scholarship, with an extended introduction and detailed footnotes commenting on the original Greek. The title of the translation, *Toledot milhemet hayehudim im haromaim* ('History of the War of the Jews with the Romans'), already signaled his determination to stick close to Josephus's text, and he was highly critical of Schulman's biblicizing style of Hebrew and frequent mistakes—even if his own translation, which aimed to be relatively literal, was not without inaccuracies.[27]

Simchoni's translation was frequently reprinted over the next few decades and became the standard version of the *Jewish War* used by Hebrew speakers, but Simchoni's championing of Josephus as man and historian was not adopted by other Hebrew scholars. Events both in Europe and in Palestine in the 1930s discouraged any leniency toward Josephus as a collaborator with Rome, and historians took for granted his moral degeneracy and his unreliability. For a generation dedicated to building a new Jewish state and embroiled in a struggle for independence from the rule of a Western imperial power, the parallels between Roman Judaea in the first century and the British Mandate were obvious, and Josephus, with his apologia for Rome, seemed to be on the wrong side of history. Thus the great historian Abraham Schalit, whose studies of Herod and Roman rule in Judaea dominated Israeli historiography of the Roman period in the early years of the Israeli state, referred in 1934 to Josephus's 'degenerate character' in scholarly articles he wrote on the 'national-political' views of Josephus in the *Jewish War*. More insidiously, Schalit simply altered the evidence in the *Jewish War* at will in his monograph on Roman rule in Judaea, published in 1936–37, when Josephus's account failed to castigate the Roman regime as Schalit took for granted should have been done. Presumably Josephus could be taken to have omitted such castigation only because of his pro-Roman proclivities. Similarly, Schalit's slightly younger colleague, Gedalyahu Alon, assumed in an article in 1938–39, on the destruction of the Temple, that Josephus's failure to blame the evil Titus for the disaster, as the rabbis did, could be explained only by Josephus employing the 'sweet talk and the slyness of a hypocrite' who wrote the truth only when he was negligent.[28]

Such blanket condemnation of Josephus and the *Jewish War* was tempered during the 1940s by a growing awareness among scholars connected to the rapidly growing Hebrew University of the value of Josephus's other writings, especially the *Antiquities*, for study of the Hellenistic period, including the revolt of the Maccabees, and of the biblical period, and recognition of the relationship of his Bible interpretations to traditions found elsewhere in Jewish literature, such as in the Septuagint, Targumim, and midrash. A major cause of this re-evaluation was the availability by the mid-1940s of two new Hebrew versions of the first half of the *Antiquities*; one of these was by Schalit, and his introduction in 1943–44 strikes a markedly different tone to his condemnation of Josephus a decade earlier: '*Antiquities* is the first work composed after the destruction of the Second Temple that envisions the future of the Jewish people in the West as a positive political programme, and Josephus was its author. . . . Nowadays, about nineteen hundred years later, we know that Josephus' plan was based upon an illusion. But we must not accuse him of "treason" and of having abandoned his people'. Daniel Schwartz has noted that Schalit omitted his earlier article of 1934 from the list of publications he submitted to the Hebrew University when he applied for an appointment in the late 1940s, and it appears that by that date Schalit had repudiated his previous hostility to acceptance of Josephus's status as a serious historian.[29]

Earlier, in 1943–44, the aged scholar Aharon (Armand) Kaminka (1866–1950), who had already in 1897 delivered a lecture in Hebrew to the first Zionist Congress on Jewish settlement in Palestine and was the first to translate Greek tragedies into Hebrew as well as the philosophical writings of Aristotle, Marcus Aurelius, and Seneca, enthused about Josephus, who 'so extolled and praised and reinforced the spirit of the Jewish people', noting that 'despite his moral failings and departures from the truth in his memories concerning his youth, we must bow our head in respect to this great man'. Once historians stopped judging Josephus as a historian solely on the basis of his account of contemporary history that was made so contentious by his own involvement, his virtues in recording the past with such devotion became more apparent. In November 1949, in an article, 'On *The Wars of the Jews*', in the popular Hebrew journal *Dorot*, Schalit, with his revised appreciation of Josephus's character, claimed (much in the style of Simchoni) that the *Jewish War* shows the Jewish historian as 'a lamenter, whose soul was linked to that of the ancient biblical lamenters [such as Jeremiah]': according to Schalit in this new, more positive mode, 'the book testifies to the suffering of its author's soul and his inner struggle. It is a worthy monument not only to the times it describes, but also to the man who produced it out of the confusion and convolution of his soul'. Of course it may also have been relevant that much had happened in the life of the Jewish nation in Europe between 1932 and 1945 to encourage greater sympathy for Josephus as witness to a national tragedy he had been powerless to prevent.

The foundation of the State of Israel in 1948 encouraged greater confidence in the *Jewish War* as a narrative for a proud new nation—and therefore provided an incentive to accept that narrative at face value, in particular when the excavation of Masada by Yigael Yadin in the early 1960s turned the siege of the fortress and the fate of its defenders into a national symbol of heroism (see below). Reports of the archaeological finds stressed to an Israeli public their remarkable congruence with the description of Masada in book 7 of the *Jewish War*, and an entire generation of Israelis in the 1960s adapted the story of mass suicide as emblematic of Zionist heroism. At the same time, the accidental congruence of the discovery of the Dead Sea Scrolls in 1947 with the establishment of the new state led to the scrolls playing a major role in the emerging ideology of the nation, with concomitant implications for the use of the *Jewish War* as a window into the world of Second Temple Judaism. The sectarian scrolls revealed Jews in the time of Josephus living a communal pietistic life with many similarities to the Essenes described in such detail in book 2 of the *Jewish War*. The biblical scholar Yehoshua Grintz published in the 1952–53 volume of the religious Zionist periodical *Sinai* a systematic comparison between texts from Qumran and Josephus's description of the Essenes, helping to establish a consensus on the identity of the Qumran sectarians that has been seriously challenged only in quite recent times. The contrast is striking between Zionist skepticism about Josephus's political narrative in the first half of the twentieth century and apparently entirely uncritical adoption of his idealized description of the Essenes at the start of the second half. In essence, Josephus's description was used to validate the newly discovered scrolls as evidence that the new State of Israel was founded on a religious heritage from two thousand years before.

The political career of Josephus himself was of course less easily co-opted into the foundation myths of the new state, but as the parallels between the freedom fighters of the first century and the struggle for independence from the British Mandate faded into history after 1948, a greater appreciation emerged among Israeli historians for Josephus as a political realist. In part this shift reflected a sobering realization in Israeli society after the Yom Kippur War in 1973 that an uncompromising adoption of military methods to achieve national goals was not obviously prudent. In a short book, titled simply *Josephus Flavius*, published on the basis of radio lectures by the Ministry of Defence in 1985 soon after the disastrous invasion of Lebanon in 1982, David Flusser argued forcefully against any depiction of Josephus as a traitor, and Flusser's colleague at the Hebrew University, Menahem Stern, who was widely acknowledged by his peers as the most influential historian of the late Second Temple period, introduced for the first time an appreciation of the difference between Josephus's attitude to Rome and that of other Roman provincials. In a whole series of publications, Stern emphasized the difference between the acceptance of the inevitability of Roman power pervasive in the *Jewish War*, and especially in the speech ascribed to King Agrippa in book 2, and enthusiasm for Roman rule as found in the speeches of Greek orators or even in the writings of the Jewish philosopher Philo.

Stern's reassessment of the *Jewish War* included a new appreciation of its literary qualities. No one before Stern had written in Hebrew with such enthusiasm about Josephus's descriptive skill and the art with which he fashioned his historical narrative. Nor had any scholar previously done so much to situate Josephus in the context of Greek historiography in the early Roman Empire. Stern's awareness of the wider cultural context of the *Jewish War* was not accidental. Born in Poland in 1925 in a religious family, he migrated to Palestine with his parents at the age of fifteen and studied classics and history at the Hebrew University and Oxford.

For over thirty years from the mid-1950s he taught in the Jewish History Department at the Hebrew University before his tragic death, murdered by a terrorist while walking to the university, in 1989. Most influential of his extensive scholarly output was the monumental collection of *Greek and Latin Authors on Jews and Judaism*, published in three volumes between 1974 and 1984 by the Israel Academy of Sciences and Humanities, a massive enterprise that required detailed knowledge and deep understanding of a vast swathe of classical literature.

Menahem Stern was thus unusually well qualified to express admiration of the *Jewish War* as an exceptional product of early imperial historiography in comparison to other literary production both in the non-Jewish culture in which Josephus lived and worked and in the context of Jewish Greek literature more generally. It is curious to learn that Stern's introduction to Josephus's works was not through Simchoni's Hebrew translation, which had been published in Warsaw two years before his birth in Bialystock, but through Schulman's older Hebrew version, which evidently retained a considerable readership. It is even more curious to learn that, elsewhere in 1930s Poland, Ben Zion Wacholder, a year senior to Stern and, after he settled in the United States, also a renowned scholar of the late Second Temple period, was introduced to the subject not through Josephus's works, whether in Hebrew, Yiddish, or any other language, but through *Sefer Yosippon*, which he began to read at the age of five.[30]

The life of *Sefer Yosippon* has evolved over the past two and a half centuries in parallel with that of the *Jewish War*, with which it has continued sometimes to be confused.

Schulman's Hebrew translation of the *Jewish War* had generally avoided direct imitation of the vocabulary of Yosippon, perhaps in part to distinguish the new Josephus of the Haskalah from the old Yosippon of rabbinic tradition, but we have seen that confusion between the two histories was common in Eastern Europe in Schulman's time, and that this confusion contributed to the acceptance of his translation of the *Jewish War* in orthodox circles.

At the beginning of the Haskalah, earlier in the nineteenth century, the new appreciation of the real Josephus seemed likely to lead to an end of interest in Yosippon. When Peter Beer (1758–1838), who was one of the first Jews to make his career as a teacher in the state-supervised German-Jewish schools in the Habsburg Empire and wrote a series of textbooks on Jewish history, turned his attention from biblical history and published in 1808 a history of the Jews in the Second Temple period 'according to Josephus Flavius', he preceded the appearance of his book by writing in the *Jüdisch-Deutsche Monatsschrift* a confident demolition, on historical-critical grounds, of the traditional Jewish view that *Sefer Yosippon* was the Hebrew version of Josephus's Greek text. In many respects Jews were simply catching up with the consensus in non-Jewish scholarship that *Sefer Yosippon* was a medieval chronicle of no independent value as a source for Second Temple history. Throughout the Middle Ages Jews might be attracted to Yosippon simply on grounds of access to the Hebrew text, in contrast to the *Jewish War*, which could be read only in Greek and Latin, which were seen as Christian languages. But as the *maskilim* and the scholars of the Wissenschaft des Judentums proclaimed the superiority of the *Jewish War* as

Josephus's real history, so too they made the *Jewish War* more accessible through translations into Hebrew and the vernacular. For those in Eastern Europe, Zelig Kalmanovitch published in Vilna a translation of the *Jewish War* into Yiddish in 1914. A socialist nationalist, Kalmanovitch called for a synthesis of Jewish and European culture in the diaspora on similar lines to Simon Dubnow, whose history of the Jews he had translated into Yiddish from Russian. Nine years earlier, Yaakov Shertok, father of Moshe Sharett (the second prime minister of Israel), had published in Saint Petersburg a Russian translation of the *Jewish War* in the interval between his first settlement in Palestine in the 1880s and his return there in 1906. Why would anyone interested in the Jewish war against Rome wish to turn to the discredited text of Yosippon?

A partial answer must lie just in the force of tradition and the large number of editions of Yosippon printed since the fifteenth century. Copies were freely available in Yiddish and other Jewish languages as well as Hebrew, and as we have seen, the rabbis approved of the text on the grounds that it had been known to the rabbinic authorities of medieval times. For some historical topics, such as the story of the Maccabees, the use of Josephus's *Antiquities* in the text of Yosippon provided a fuller and more inspiring narrative than the brief version in book 1 of the *Jewish War*, as well as tantalizing glimpses into aspects of the history of other nations such as the Alexander Romance and snippets of early Roman traditions. Not the least important was the continued popularity of Amelander's Yiddish history *Sheyris Yisrael* ('The Remnant of Israel'), published as a supplement to the Yosippon ('the second part', as it was proclaimed in the title page), bringing Jewish history up to the modern age. An abridged Hebrew translation of Amelander's edition, published in 1804, was reprinted several times, and a new edition in 1846 by the Lemberg *maskil* Abraham Menachem Mendel Mohr brought the history up to date with an account of the Damascus Affair of 1840, when the Jews of Damascus had been rescued, after much suffering, from an accusation of ritual murder. We have seen similar updating of Josephus's own histories in some of the numerous editions of Whiston's English translation published around the same time as Mohr's updating of *Sheyris Yisrael*, but without any indication of the author of the new material. None of the Jewish editions of Josephus's own works in Hebrew or Yiddish seems to have followed the same practice.[31]

Whatever the cause, the continued popularity of Yosippon down to the twentieth century is not in doubt. The preface by Hayim Hominer to the 1955 edition (in Jerusalem) of his publication of the traditional Hebrew text, complete with commentary, continued to present *Sefer Yosippon* as the original text to which Josephus referred in book 1 of the *Jewish War*. Hominer's edition continues to reach a large religious readership, particularly in the days leading up to the annual fast of the Ninth of Av. Neither Hominer nor his readers were interested in the consensus of the first generation of historians in the Hebrew University, led by Joseph Klausner, that the book is without value as an independent historical source. Nor were they interested in the insistence of Yitzak Baer, a younger contemporary of Klausner at the university, that the real interest of *Sefer Yosippon* lay in investigating it as a medieval composition. It was to be Baer's student, David Flusser, who eventually brought study of the book into the mainstream of medieval studies through publication of a scholarly edition in 1980–81 based on a thorough examination of the earliest manuscripts to which he had access.

Some of the enduring attraction of *Sefer Yosippon* for many Jews may well have been the literary qualities of the work and in particular its Hebrew style. Many neologisms and idiosyncratic phrases that reflected developments in Hebrew in southern Italy from the late eighth century were adopted in the late nineteenth century by Eliezer ben Yehudah in the dictionary by means of which he sought a revival of Hebrew as a secular language. It seems to have been Yosippon's version of the Masada story, which portrayed the Jewish defenders heroically attacking the Roman troops until vanquished rather than committing suicide, on which Yitzhak Lamdan based the climax of his dramatic epic poem *Masada*, composed between 1923 and 1926 when Lamdan was in his mid-twenties, in which a refugee makes his way to the Land of Israel to take part in the final revolt against the fate of the Jews. The poem was hugely influential for Zionists through to the 1950s, not least as a school text, with particular lines set to music, and 'Masada shall not fall again' became a powerful slogan.[32]

It may also have been from Yosippon that Abba Kovner, also a poet and leader of the partisans in Vilna, borrowed on the night of 31 December 1941, in his manifesto to the Jewish youth of the ghetto, the repeated motto 'Let us not go like sheep to the slaughter', a phrase ascribed by the author of *Sefer Yosippon* to the Hasmonean patriarch Mattathias in the context of the Maccabean revolt. For Zionists in the first half of the twentieth century, Yosippon represented Jewish heroism. Hence the choice of the emotional *maskil* Micha Josef Berdyczewski, born in 1865 in the Ukraine in a Hasidic family, to adopt in 1914 the surname 'Bin-Gorion', which was to be inscribed on his tombstone in the Jewish cemetery in Berlin on his death in 1921. In 1912, two years before Berdyczewski, a younger contemporary, David Grün (from Plonsk in Poland), who had migrated in his late teens to Palestine but at the time was in his mid-twenties and studying law at Istanbul University, similarly adopted a new name in honor of the purported author of *Sefer Yosippon*, Joseph ben Gorion; as David Ben-Gurion, he was to be the first prime minister of the State of Israel.[33]

Micha Berdyczewski was a hugely prolific author in Yiddish and German as well as in Hebrew, publishing numerous novels, short stories, and essays, and dedicating himself to Jewish spiritual renewal through integration with the contemporary culture of the non-Jewish world, particularly in Germany, where he was deeply influenced himself by the philosophy of Nietzsche and Hegel. In Germany he was best known for his compilations of Jewish legends, retold in attractive anthologies, and his intellectual pursuits are striking in the breadth of interests they display, but he was also committed to an independent, often subversive, interpretation of Jewish history, portraying himself as a reincarnation of such freethinkers as Uriel Acosta and Baruch Spinoza. It was not at all obvious that he would choose to redefine himself by adopting the purported name of the author of *Sefer Yosippon*.[34]

In an autobiographical short story titled 'On a Long Road', Berdyczewski described his first encounter with Yosippon as a decisive spur to his imagination. The worn copy he bought with his pocket money as a young boy set him to dreaming about Jewish history from earliest times to the destruction of the Temple by the Romans, and Yosippon continued to fascinate for the rest of his life. According to his son, Emanuel bin Gorion, who dedicated himself to the preservation of his father's literary and scholarly reputation, Berdyczewski chose the new family name in full awareness of the complex relationship between Yosef ben Gurion, to whom *Sefer Yosippon* was traditionally attributed, and Yosef ben Mattityahu, the historical Josephus, and he aimed to capitalize on the ambiguity: 'Bin Gorion' was meant to be both the rebel leader mentioned by Josephus in book 2 of the *Jewish War*, as commander in Jerusalem alongside the former High Priest Hanan ben Hanan, and the historian Josephus on whose writings Berdyczewski believed could be founded significant new insights not only into Jewish history but into the origins of Christianity.[35]

The most dramatic of these novel insights, published by Berdyczewski's son Emanuel as *Yeshu ben Hanan* nearly forty years after his father's death, was the claim that the prophet Jesus son of Ananias, whose career in the seven years leading up to the destruction of Jerusalem was described by Josephus in book 6 of the *Jewish War*, was the real Jesus whose life formed the foundation of the Christian faith. This Jesus was a pious, peace-loving rustic who had been blessed with a premonition of the destruction of Jerusalem and had been mocked and eventually executed for his prophecy. The presentation of the argument, replete with references to a vast swathe of ancient and medieval Jewish sources, failed to persuade scholars when it was issued to the public by Emanuel bin Gorion in 1959, for the good reason that it combined dismissal of the entire Gospel tradition as tendentious legend with exceptional confidence in the historicity of the main elements of Josephus's account in the *Jewish War* (although Josephus himself had stated that Jesus son of Ananias was not executed by the Jerusalem authorities, and that he died when hit by a *ballista* ball at the height of the Roman siege). Emanuel was exceptionally prickly in his dedicated protection of the image of his father as a prophetic sage, and his fury at the rejection by scholars of *Yeshu ben Hanan*, which he ascribed to religious conservatism, was not assuaged by recognition of its literary merits.[36]

Emanuel had laid the foundations for the faith in Josephus's historical reliability which was required for acceptance of his father's theory by publishing already in 1933 a carefully manipulated presentation of Josephus as a man. *Das Leben des Flavius Josephus*, published by Schocken in Berlin, was a translation into German of Josephus's first-person account of his background and career as written by Josephus in the beginning and end of his *Life*, with the central section of the book comprising Josephus's third-person account of his career as found in the *Jewish War*. This combination of sources was contrived to present Josephus as a more decisive figure than would have appeared from a simple translation of the more apologetic narrative of his behavior during the Galilee campaign provided by Josephus in the *Life*. Not that Josephus was entirely heroic in the *Jewish War* account: to improve further the image of his hero, Emanuel doctored Josephus's speeches at Jotapata and before the wall of Jerusalem by excision of passages that might place Josephus in an unfavorable light, such as his vow to his comrades in book 3 (3.381) not to defect to the enemy (as, of course, he did soon afterward). Bin Gorion's positive evaluation of the *Jewish War* as a historical source and of Josephus's literary talent was shared with Jacob Simchoni, the translator of the *Jewish War* into Hebrew, who had known Berdyczewski and, in the book's introduction, thanked him, as 'the great admirer of Flavius Josephus', 'for supporting me in toiling on this book's translation during the last year of his life, before the untimely setting of his sun; he was the first to read my translation in manuscript and to congratulate me on the final outcome'. As we have seen, in Zionist circles at least in the 1920s, both Simchoni and Bin Gorion were swimming against a strong current of suspicion in such championing of Josephus and his best known book.[37]

Such a disparity of views about Josephus and his testimony to the last days of the Second Temple spawned in the 1930s and 1940s a number of literary reactions in which the depiction of the ancient author stood proxy for an analysis of the current turmoil in Jewish life both in Europe and in Palestine. In 1930 the idiosyncratic Yekhiel Yeshaye Trunk, a Polish Jew of considerable wealth who threw himself with fervor into the diaspora socialism of the Bund and embraced Greek philosophy and psychoanalysis even as he established himself as a leading figure within the Yiddish Writers Union in Warsaw, titled a book of Yiddish short stories 'Josephus Flavius from Jerusalem and Other Historical Novels', and in 1932 Lion Feuchtwanger published the first volume of his trilogy of historical novels that dominated perceptions of Josephus in the eyes of the general Jewish public in the middle of the twentieth century, not least through adaptation as plays.[38]

Lion Feuchtwanger (1884–1958), from a middle-class orthodox German Jewish family, was a prominent playwright and historical novelist in Weimar Germany who was closely associated with the young Bertolt Brecht. His novel *Jew Süss*, based on the life of Joseph Süss Oppenheimer, published in 1925, went through five printings in its first year and by 1931 had been translated into seventeen languages. By the early 1930s his literary reputation was thus secure, but his vociferous opposition to the new regime made him an early victim of the Nazi rise to power, and in the summer of 1933 he was one of the first Jews to be deprived of German citizenship and rendered stateless. His decision to focus for the next decade specifically on Josephus's dilemmas when confronted by the might of imperial Rome closely reflected the quandary into which he, like other European Jews, had been thrust.

The first novel in the trilogy, published in German in 1932 with the title *Die Jüdische Krieg* but with the title *Josephus: A Historical Romance* in English the following year, closely followed the narrative of Josephus's life in his own works, but with the addition of imaginary scenes as illustration of the private life of the young Judaean priest Yosef ben Matityahu. The second volume (*Die Söhne* ['The Sons'] in German but *The Jew of Rome* in English) traced the new life of the historian as Flavius Josephus, imagined as a well-known citizen of Rome. Already in the first volume, Josephus was portrayed as celebrating his life in Alexandria as a survivor of the Judaean disaster and as composing a 'psalm', that 'would later be called . . . "A Psalm for the Citizen of the World"', which quite brazenly celebrated Jewish life in the diaspora:

Praise God and be ye dispersed among the nations.
Praise God and scatter yourselves over the seas.
Praise God and lose yourselves in infinite spaces.
A slave is he who binds himself to a single country.
The Kingdom that I promise you, its name is not Zion.
Its name is the earth.

Both these first two volumes of the trilogy were translated into Hebrew almost immediately after the German
publication and published in Tel Aviv with the titles *War of
the Jews* for volume 1 and *The Sons* for volume 2. Perhaps
unsurprisingly a reviewer in *Moznayim* in November 1932
took the author to task for producing diaspora literature
with 'exile motifs' that 'falsify the ancient realities of our
people'. It may be significant that the reviewer, the young
historian Ephraim Shmueli, who was only then emigrating
from Poland to Palestine in his mid-twenties, titled his review *Milhamot hayehudim* ('Wars of the Jews'), reverting to
the plural 'wars' that had been adopted by Schulman for his
Hebrew version of Josephus's history but had been dropped
both in the new translation by Simchoni and in the title of
Feuchtwanger's novel.[39]

The second volume of Feuchtwanger's trilogy included a
new 'psalm' that went beyond claiming the earth in place of
Zion to proclaim that all that matters is the individual self:
'Why must I, being Joseph Ben Matthias, become also a
Roman or a Jew or both together? I will be myself, I will be
Joseph'. Feuchtwanger had settled in the south of France following his exile from Germany, but he was dismayed at the
supine attitude toward the Nazis in the West and flirted
with the Soviet Union, publishing in 1937 an account of a

visit to Moscow the previous winter in which he seems to have fallen for Stalinist propaganda. On the outbreak of war he was interned in a camp in the commune of Aix-en-Provence, eventually escaping via Marseille to seek asylum in America. But by the time that he published from his exile in America in 1942 the third and final volume of the Josephus trilogy, in London under the English title *The Day Will Come* (the title also used in the Hebrew edition published in Tel Aviv in 1945) and in New York as *Josephus and the Emperor*, such individualism seemed far too optimistic. The story of Josephus in the Rome of Domitian, portrayed as a ferment of anti-Jewish sentiment engendered not least by the threat to the Roman religious order posed by the rabbis of Yavneh and nascent Christianity, destroyed all hope of such an abolition of ethnic boundaries. The trilogy ends with Josephus returning to Judaea as an old man and seeking to join the new messianism of Rabbi Akiba, only to die at the hands of a Roman soldier.

It is hard not to see the arc of hope and despair across the three books as a reflection of Feuchtwanger's predicament and that of European Jewry as a whole. Certainly reviews of the final book in 1944 in the Hebrew press in Palestine welcomed Feuchtwanger, like the hero of his novel, as a penitent who had returned to the bosom of his people and recognized the power of nationalist dreams.[40]

Feuchtwanger's background as a playwright in Weimar Berlin may have encouraged him to promote, already in November 1933, the adaptation for the stage of the first volume of his Josephus trilogy. Scripted by Maurice Schwartz and staged by the Yiddish Art Theater of New York, the play in two acts was spectacular, with over a hundred actors.

Schwartz himself took the lead role as Josephus. The division into twenty-two scenes suggests that his script may have tried to include too much of the novel to make for a satisfactory drama, but the *New York Times* was enthusiastic, describing the production as 'a credit to the Yiddish Art Company and its director'. The paper was explicit in linking Schwartz's play to Feuchtwanger, 'one of the most skillful of historical novelists', but Feuchtwanger's influence on other theater productions about Josephus in the 1930s and 1940s was also real if less blatant. Thus, for instance, in 1938 the Hebrew play *Jerusalem and Rome* by Nathan Bistritsky, who adopted the Hebrew name Agmon, showed Josephus meeting Yohanan ben Zakkai outside Jerusalem and imploring him to return to the city to try to stop the insanity of the rebels. Bistritsky, originally from Russia, had encountered considerable success in 1931 with a dramatization of the life of Shabbetai Zevi, and this new play was praised for its depiction of Berenice as genuinely in love with Titus and as responsible for trying to prevent the destruction of the Temple by Roman troops, a motif almost certainly borrowed from the first volume of Feuchtwanger's trilogy, published five years before the play, which had contained the earliest representation of Berenice as an independent political actor and as an essentially heroic tragic character.[41]

Two reviewers in the popular newspaper *Davar* praised Bistritsky's play for its dramatic power on the page, and on 8 September 1939 Ephraim Tzoref specifically noted Bistritsky's courage in presenting Joseph Ben Matityahu as motivated by noble altruism rather than by self-interest as standardly presumed in contemporary Zionist historiography. But the play was less successful when produced with a star cast by Habimah in Tel Aviv in 1941. With the Second World War at its height, the message of the play, that compromise with Rome may be advisable for the greater good, could too easily be seen as a covert call to the Jews of Palestine to restrain their struggle against the British Mandate for the greater aim of victory, as advocated by Labour Zionists. Such political messages could expect a mixed response from a theater audience. Much of the acting was praised, but one reviewer, the translator and journalist Baruch Krupnik (Karu), complained in *Haaretz* that the great actor Shimon Finkel, who played Josephus, had failed to live up to the playwright's depiction of the historian and had fallen back into familiar clichés in his portrayal.[42]

The international prestige of Feuchtwanger's novels was sufficient already in 1935 for the Russian composer Moshe Milner in Leningrad to base his Yiddish opera *Josephus Flavius* on the first volume of the trilogy (although I was unable to track down evidence that it was ever performed). In 1947 a radio play titled *The Jewish War*, which was aired on *Kol Yisrael*, the only Hebrew radio station in operation at the time, was also based on the first novel of the trilogy rather than Josephus's own writings. But other contemporary dramas about Josephus came more directly from Josephus's own works. Many of these dramas were very slight, but among the more powerful was *The Cave of Josephus*, a portrayal of Josephus at Jotapata by Shalom Joseph Schapira, a Hebrew poet originally from Poland who took the pen name Shin Shalom; the play, originally published in 1934–35, was sufficiently noticed to be reissued in revised form in 1956. In a play titled *Among the Shepherds: A Night in the Environs of Jerusalem*, by Itzhak Katzelson, a poet originally from Karelitz in Belarus, Josephus appears as a character alongside other heroes of Jewish history, such as King Saul, Daniel, and Solomon Molcho. Published first in Hebrew in 1931 but later expanded and translated into Yiddish, the play was performed in the Warsaw Ghetto in 1941, where Katzelson was a leading ideologue of the uprising. In such a context the respect paid to Josephus for his role in preserving national memory is striking.[43]

Feuchtwanger, who spent his last fifteen years in California, is thought to have attempted unsuccessfully to break into films, and in view of the close involvement of many Jews in Hollywood, it is curious that the *Jewish War* was so rarely depicted on screen during the twentieth century. The rebuff to Feuchtwanger may have reflected his reputation during the Joseph McCarthy era as a communist sympathizer—it would not have helped that in 1953 he was awarded the National Prize of East Germany for art and literature. When the story of Masada was eventually filmed, it was as a television miniseries, originally aired in four episodes on ABC in April 1981, and based on the epic novel *The Antagonists*, published in 1971 by Ernest Gann as an exploration of the contrasting ideals of the Roman general Lucius Flavius Silva and the Jewish rebel leader Eleazar ben Yair. Gann was a prolific and popular non-Jewish novelist from the American Midwest whose fiction was best known for its frequent description of aviation, to which he devoted much of his life. He seems to have lacked any interest in the issues of authenticity that troubled contemporary Jewish readers of the Masada narrative in book 7 of the *Jewish War*, and many of the best scenes, such as the role of the Jewish mistress of Silva, were pure invention. But the series was a success in large part because of the acting of Peter O'Toole and David Warner and the photogenic qualities of the Masada site, where the episodes were filmed, and a feature-length version was eventually released for home viewing. ABC was concerned that the background to the story would be unknown to a general American audience and commissioned a factual documentary, also starring O'Toole, to tell a version of the history of the Jewish revolt against Rome. For most American viewers the story resonated less with ideas about the Jewish national past than with the pictures on their televisions of the contemporary conflict between Israel and the Palestinians.

If the site of Masada struck a chord with viewers this will have been the result of the remarkable international publicity that surrounded the excavations on the site by Yigael Yadin in the mid-1960s. The site itself had been identified already in 1838 by the Americans Edward Robinson and Eli Smith. Recourse to the *Jewish War* was common among Christian visitors to sites in the Holy Land during the nineteenth century, and the book featured prominently in the private travel diary of Judith Montefiore following her first visit to Jerusalem with her husband Moses in 1827, presumably as a result of recourse to Christian travel guides. By the late 1920s the striking profile of the mountain against the background of the desert and Dead Sea had turned the rock into a focus of pilgrimage for Zionist Jews fired up by the rhetoric of Yitzhak Lamdan's poem. The visit to the site took on an extra meaning for the students from Zionist high schools who arrived only after a grueling journey on foot through the desert; there was a temporary pause after a devastating earthquake hit the northern Dead Sea region in

FIGURE 4.3 Masada. The site of the mass suicide of Sicarii according to book 7 of the *Jewish War*. Photo, courtesy of Andrew Shiva.

July 1927, but during the 1930s the pilgrimage featured regularly in the program of Zionist youth movements.[44]

Chief among those responsible for building up the Masada myth was the amateur archaeologist Shmaryahu Guttman. Guttman, born to Russian Jewish parents, had migrated to Palestine from Scotland in 1912 as a young child. In his late teens he became a kibbutznik and farmer, but as a Zionist activist in his early twenties, he dedicated himself to investigating the land of Israel, including the fortress of Masada, which he climbed in 1933. Guttman had no formal archaeological training, but he had enthusiasm and a good knowledge of the text of book 7 of the *Jewish War*, which had recently been published in Hebrew by Simchoni, and it was Guttman who discovered the 'snake path' used by the ancient Jewish defenders to reach the summit of the rock. To turn Masada into a national symbol, Guttman read the Josephus text selectively, ignoring the unhelpful depiction of the defenders of the fortress as Sicarii who had played only a minimal role in opposition to Rome and had preyed on their fellow Jews in Ein Gedi. Calling them 'Zealots', as Guttman did, directly contradicted Josephus, who explicitly distinguished zealots from *sicarii* precisely in his account of the defense of Masada, but 'Zealot' sounded heroic—and Guttman could assume that few visitors to the site would have read Josephus's description of the Masada siege in the *Jewish War* (7.252–406) with sufficient attention to note the vituperation against the Zealots embedded within it (7.268–74).

Guttman's enthusiasm for the Masada myth mushroomed through the increasingly dangerous years of the 1930s, and in January 1942 he convened a five-day seminar, attended by a large group of Zionist leaders, to discuss exploitation of the site through archaeological investigations, as well as exploitation of Lamdan's poem and Josephus's *Jewish War*. The seminar set the pattern for future visits to the site through the 1940s by youth groups and by the soldiers of the Palmach, for whom the desert hike, through potentially hostile territory, functioned as military training. Nocturnal ceremonies were devised to celebrate the heroism of the ancient Jews who had fought and died on the rock. After the foundation of the State of Israel, hikes by school and youth movements continued through the fifties: now far less dangerous, they were often concluded by a dramatic reading of the final oration by Eleazar ben Yair (7.341–88), delivered just before his heroic death along with his comrades, and for a while there was a tradition in the Armoured Corps of the Israel Defense Forces established by the new state after 1948 for new recruits to be sworn in at the site.

The significance of the seminar in 1942 in establishing the Masada myth was recognized in 2012 by the organization of another seminar on Masada to mark its seventieth anniversary. By now, the official relationship of the site to Josephus's account in the *Jewish War* was enshrined in a museum, opened in 2007 at the foot of the mountain, and in a sound and light show that reenacted the Masada story: the show imagined Josephus explaining to Lucius Flavius Silva that the Jews on the rock were celebrating the Passover Seder—reinforcing the standard Jewish view that Josephus was a voice from the Roman side of the conflict despite the impossibility that he could himself have witnessed the siege, since by the time the siege began he was ensconced far away in Rome.[45]

When Yigael Yadin began his extensive excavations at Masada between 1963 and 1965, the site was thus already totemic. Guttman, who had undertaken a small investigatory dig in 1959, was co-opted onto Yadin's team. Extensive funding was sought successfully from abroad, with an appeal led by the *Observer* newspaper in London for volunteers to participate in the enterprise, and the result was the largest archaeological dig in the world, with hundreds of people, mostly young, from all over the world entranced by the mystique of the desert and the isolation despite the basic conditions in which they were housed. The whole operation was a major logistical achievement, and a public relations triumph carefully nurtured by David Astor, editor of the *Observer*, who printed regular reports from the dig from a 'special correspondent', who was probably Yadin himself. By 1966 much of Herod's fortress had been uncovered, and Masada had become a household name across the world, bringing with it the reputation of Josephus and the *Jewish War* as the source from which the romance of Masada was felt to derive.

The archaeologist responsible for this international attention was no ordinary scholar. By the mid-1960s, Yigael Yadin was in his mid-fifties and a powerful figure within the Israeli establishment. His father, Eleazar Sukenik, had come to Palestine from Poland in 1912 and established the Department of Archaeology at the Hebrew University, but Yadin's own career as an archaeologist began only after a glittering military career before and after the establishment of the State of Israel, culminating in three years as chief of staff of the Israel Defense Forces between 1949 and 1952. Much of his success in coordinating a project as large as the Masada excavation can be attributed to his military expertise and his contacts with former military colleagues who provided practical assistance.

Yadin was to conduct other major excavations in ensuing years, but none quite on the scale of Masada. He was a brilliant scholar and organizer, but he was also a politician with a serious sense of mission for the nascent state, evinced eventually in the mid-1990s by the creation of a new political party and a spell as deputy prime minister. His publication of the Masada finds in English in 1966 adopted Guttman's description of Masada's defenders as 'Zealots', claiming to have uncovered the site of 'Herod's Fortress and the Zealots' last stand'. The misreading of Josephus can hardly have been an accident for a scholar with outstanding expertise in textual analysis who had already, in 1956, received the Israel Prize for his doctoral thesis on the Dead Sea Scrolls.

Yadin's insistence that his excavations confirmed the truth of Josephus's report of the heroism of the defenders, down to interpretation of a potsherd discovered with the name 'ben Yair' as testimony to the drawing of lots before the mass suicide, may have been selective, but it was hugely effective in promoting more extensive use of the *Jewish War* for identifying other features of the archaeological landscape. The site of Jotapata, where Josephus surrendered to Vespasian, had already been identified in 1847 by the German archaeologist Ernst Gustav Schultz on the basis of Josephus's description in the *Jewish War*, but it was only in the 1990s that extensive excavation revealed much evidence of the siege, including a mass grave. After identification in 1968 of Gamala with the site of Tell es Salam on the Golan, northeast of Lake Tiberias, as part of the archaeological survey of the region following the Six-Day War, from 1977 to 2000 Shmaryahu Guttman led excavations, in conjunction with Danny Syon, on behalf of the Israeli Department of Antiquities, confirming the extent of the battle through a great wealth of finds, including large numbers of arrowheads and ballista stones.

The archaeologists themselves often express caution about the correlation between their finds and the evidence of the *Jewish War*, particularly with regard to numbers, which appear to have been routinely exaggerated by Josephus, but tourist guides (and many information boards at the sites) are less inhibited. When Josephus's descriptions of the country are doubted even by the guides, it is not because he is deemed intrinsically untrustworthy (as in the Zionist view in the 1930s of his political stance) but because his testimony is contradicted by other evidence accorded greater credence. Thus both the model reconstruction of the Temple and its environs in the late Second Temple period which was created by Michael Avi-Yonah in the 1960s for the Holyland Hotel and is now in the Israel Museum and the model set up ca. 2000 by the Western Wall Heritage Foundation for visitors to the tunnels alongside the Western Wall of the Temple prefer the evidence of the Mishnah to that of Josephus in the reconstruction of the Temple building, although the Avi-Yonah model gives primacy to Josephus's description in the reconstruction of the Temple Mount as a whole. Josephus's credibility with regard to the Temple itself is not helped by the differences between his accounts of the structure in the *Jewish War* and in the *Antiquities*, perhaps reflecting changes to the building in the more than eighty years between its original construction by Herod the Great and its destruction in 70 CE.

It is a measure of the increased respect during the 1960s of religious Zionists for Josephus's testimony in the *Jewish War* that the first authority to use Josephus's narrative as support for an opinion on a matter of *halakha* (Jewish law) was the warrior rabbi Shlomo Goren, who, as chief rabbi of the Israel Defense Forces, led the first Jewish prayers at the

Western Wall on 7 June 1967 after the capture of East Jerusalem and courted controversy by seeking to establish regular Jewish prayer meetings on the Temple Mount itself. Before Goren, no rabbinic authority since antiquity seems ever to have cited Josephus, but in 1960 Goren explicitly cited the 'heroism of Masada in the light of the primary sources' as an argument in favor of the permissibility of suicide in circumstances when the women would be led into prostitution and the men put to an agonizing death if they did not kill themselves. The coincidence of this intervention with the plans for excavation of the site by Yigael Yadin is unlikely to have been accidental. It is striking that for Goren the narrative of the defense of Masada in the *Jewish War* was preferred to that of *Sefer Yosippon*, to which he did not refer. It is also striking that he took for granted the reliability of Josephus's tragic story as a direct report of a historical event, as did those rabbis (notably Moshe Tzvi Neriah) who argued vehemently against Goren's halakhic view, examining in detail the wording attributed by Josephus to Eleazar ben Yair in his last speech.[46]

It might seem that, with its use for such purposes, the *Jewish War* had decisively entered into the canon of authoritative Jewish literature, but such a conclusion would be premature. The continuing ambivalence of Israelis was summed up toward the end of his life in the poem 'Yosefus', published in the 1980s by the poet Yitzhak Shalev, who had spent years referring to Josephus in his role as a tour guide:

> The paths in the books of times
> Lead to Josephus.
> Footnotes say: 'See in Josephus'.

Without him there is no first nor second wall,
Neither upper nor lower city,
No Temple, Antonia
And Herod.

And Eleazar Ben Yair's speech
Read to my youths ascending Masada
To the light of torches—
It, also, would not exist.

Accompanying me like a shadow on the wall,
Guiding me to Phasael tower,
He leads me to the hump of Gamla
And on the Yodfat path,
In my rucksack, on my back
— *The Wars of the Jews*.

Year after year he stands trial before me,
And my hand, reaching out to seal his fate,
Is suddenly stilled.
The verdict has been suspended
To a later date . . .[47]

The Present and Future of the *Jewish War*

The past few decades have seen an explosion of scholarship on the *Jewish War* that shows no signs of abating. In Israel, the work of Menahem Stern in the 1970s stimulated a new generation of historians. In France Pierre Vidal-Naquet, a leading historian of ancient Greece who acquired a high public profile as a campaigner against deliberate falsehoods disseminated by the state, especially with regard to the use of torture by the French army, brought Josephus into the center of his concerns to trace the relation between memory, history, and truth in an influential and provocative essay, 'Du bon usage de la trahison' ('On the Right Use of Treason'), published in 1977. The essay explored the inevitability of the historian being an 'eternal traitor' and emphasized the positive value in Josephus's account of the Jewish past despite its overall tragic theme. As a teenager, Vidal-Naquet had lost both his parents in Auschwitz, and in the 1980s he had both fiercely attacked the 'assassins of memory' who denied the Holocaust and campaigned for truth in modern Jewish history, presenting himself as an intellectual French Jewish patriot dedicated to the truth like those who had fought for the reputation of Alfred Dreyfus in the previous century. His positive appraisal of Josephus as historian despite his political treachery was seen as significant by him as well as by others—he noted that he hoped just to be a 'more subtle traitor'.[1]

For readers of German, the publication in 1961 of *Die Zeloten* by Martin Hengel, who was to devote his theological studies to understanding early Christianity within the context of Judaism in the first century CE, brought the evidence of the *Jewish War* to the attention of a new generation of New Testament scholars. But the greatest fillip to Josephus scholarship in these years was in the English-speaking world, where a series of ancient historians began to recognize the extraordinary value of the *Jewish War* as a unique account of the travails of a provincial Roman society in the early imperial period as witnessed by the provincials themselves. The rediscovery of Josephus as a source for Roman history owed much to a widening of perspective in the study of Roman history, to incorporate the Near East and minority cultures both within and neighboring the Roman world, by Arnaldo Momigliano and Fergus Millar in England and by Glen Bowersock and Erich Gruen in the United States. As the level of expertise in classical languages among the general population has declined, so has the attraction of an approach to the ancient world primarily through analysis of a long-established canon of Greek and Latin literature. Among the many alternative approaches that have come into vogue in more recent years has been a focus on less traditional literature—including Josephus. In the 1970s and 1980s Shaye Cohen, Tessa Rajak, and Per Bilde published investigations into the literary qualities of the *Jewish War* and the *Life* in light of contemporary historiography, which effectively brought an end within scholarship to assertions of a moral link between Josephus's alleged political treachery and his role as a historian. At the same time a burgeoning interest in the background to early Christianity among New Testament scholars has led to a plethora of studies on the use of the *Jewish War* to reconstruct the social and political tensions in Galilee and Judaea in the time of Jesus. All such studies were placed on a new foundation by the astonishing industry of Louis Feldman at Yeshiva University in New York, whose bibliographical publications in particular opened up a plethora of topics for further investigation. Feldman taught classics at Yeshiva University for sixty-two years, from 1955 to his death in 2017 at the age of ninety-one, devoting himself throughout his career to presenting Josephus's writings as crucial in understanding Jewish interactions with Greek culture in the Roman period. His prolific publications dominated the growing world of Josephus scholarship for much of the second half of the twentieth century.[2]

By the end of that century, Feldman's positivist approach to Josephus was increasingly criticized by a younger generation of classicists and ancient historians, including many of his former students. It was not enough anymore just to treat the *Jewish War* as part of the corpus of classical Greek texts, to be edited and construed. The book needed to be read as literature, and its idiosyncrasies explained using techniques honed in the study of the postcolonialist literatures of more recent empires. Situating the *Jewish War* within the context of the wider literature of the Flavian period has led some scholars to detect irony in his praise of Vespasian and Titus. Since the 1980s Josephus has been frequently interpreted against the background of the Greek cultural resistance to

Roman rule enshrined in the writings of the so-called Second Sophistic, which harked back to the glories of classical Athens. In more recent decades he has also been seen as a specifically Roman writer, with some scholars seeking evidence of intertextuality with other writers in Flavian Rome, although the extent of his familiarity with Latin literature—and, indeed, his ability to understand Latin—remains debated. It is unlikely that such issues will be resolved in the immediate future, but the gradual publication under the editorship of Steve Mason of a very detailed commentary on the *Jewish War* in English translation, of which the first volume (on book 2) appeared in 2007, is likely to encourage more detailed studies of Josephus's rhetorical techniques in the sophisticated manipulation of his readers. The decision to give the book the title *Judaean War* reflects Mason's distinctive stance in a continuing controversy as to whether the correct translation of the Greek word *ioudaios* should be 'Jew' (referring to religion) or 'Judaean' (referring to place of origin), an issue of particular significance in the interpretation of the term in the Gospel of John. The publication in 2009 of a superb new translation by Lisa Ulmann of the *Jewish War* into contemporary literary Hebrew, with an introduction by Jonathan Price and extensive notes by Israel Shatzman, can be expected to have a similar impact on Israeli scholars—as Price notes, 'in the *Jewish War* we read about the vicissitudes in the life of Josephus and about the events to which he was a witness as though we were looking over his shoulder . . . and we experience them together with him. He tells a riveting tale and weaves a spellbinding plot'.[3]

The spell cast by Josephus and his tale continues to have different effects on readers in accordance with their cultural and political predispositions. In 1973, the composer Yosef Tal, who taught in the Musicology Department in the Hebrew University, combined electronic sounds with conventional instruments in his opera *Masada* in a fashion considered very avant-garde at the time. A pamphlet on 'The True Authorship of the New Testament', published in 1979 by an American conspiracy theorist who called himself Abelard Reuchlin, claimed that the Gospels were written by the Roman aristocrat Arius Calpurnius Piso as a form of social control and that Piso had taken the pen name 'Flavius Josephus'. The political playwright Yehoshua Sobol aroused strong reactions when his drama titled *War of the Jews*, which used the story from Josephus to probe tensions in contemporary Israeli society, was staged in Haifa in 1981. The novelist Frederic Raphael in 2013 reimagined Josephus sympathetically as the prototype of an un-Jewish Jew and assimilated intellectual constantly haunted by his survival and the imperative to report news that no one wants to hear, reflecting on what he saw as the relationship between his own status as an assimilated Jew and the role of Josephus between Jerusalem and Rome. A novel by Alice Hoffman, published in 2011, adopts Josephus's narrative in a story about the sufferings of four women during the siege of Masada. The book was adapted for television and broadcast in the United States in 2015, with the actor Sam Neill portraying Josephus.[4]

The continuing life of the *Jewish War* may be best encapsulated by the film *La guerre des fils de lumière contre les fils des ténèbres* ('The War of the Sons of Light against the Sons of Darkness'), shown at the Venice Biennale in 1993 and at the Avignon Festival in 2009. The film records a stage production of a play by Amos Gitai, an Israeli filmmaker whose critical, often angry, analyses of Israeli society and the conflict with the Palestinians has aroused such hostility in his native country that he has spent many years in self-imposed exile in France. Gitai has referred to Josephus as 'one of my ghosts'. The film presents a reading of the *Jewish War* by the actress Jeanne Moreau, describing the revolt, the fall of Jerusalem, and the siege of Masada, with Josephus's text interspersed with biblical quotations (mostly from Lamentations) and the rabbinic prayer for the dead. Even after so many years and so many different readings, the *Jewish War* still has the power to move.[5]

Passages with a Life of Their Own

[1.1–3] *Josephus's introduction to his history, with his claim to have written an earlier version*

The war fought by the Jews against the Romans was not only the greatest war of our time but could well be one of the greatest collisions between states or nations of which word has come down to us. The historians of this war fall into two categories: those who had no part in the events have gathered from hearsay a random collection of inconsistent stories and made a rhetorical exercise of them; whereas the participants distort the facts either to flatter the Romans or out of hatred for the Jews, and in their writings you will find denunciation here, glorification there, but historical accuracy nowhere. I have therefore taken it on myself to publish to the inhabitants of the Roman Empire a Greek translation of the factual account which I had earlier written in my native language and circulated to the non-Greek speakers in the interior. I am Josephus, son of Matthias, a Hebrew by race, a native of Jerusalem, and a priest. I myself fought against the Romans in the early stages of the war, and had no choice but to witness the later events.

It is certainly not my intention to counter this Roman bias with an equally tendentious account in favour of my compatriots. I shall record the actions of both sides with strict impartiality, but my comments on the events will owe something to my own situation, and I shall allow personal sympathies the expression of sorrow at the fate that befell my country. It was destroyed by internal strife, and the responsibility for causing the reluctant intervention of Roman force and the firing of the temple lies with the Jewish warlords. Witness Titus Caesar himself: he ultimately sacked the city, but throughout the war he showed concern for the ordinary people who were kept subject to the partisans, and several times deliberately delayed the capture of the city to allow time for the guilty parties to change their mind. If any critic carps at what I say in condemnation of the warlords and their terrorist network, or in lament for my country's misfortunes, I would ask him to forget the rules of historical propriety and understand my emotion. Of all the cities in the Roman Empire ours was the one to reach the greatest heights of prosperity and then plummet to the lowest depths of misery. In fact, looking over the whole sweep of history, I would say that the sufferings of the Jews have been greater than those of any other nation—and no foreign power is to blame. Impossible, then, to hold back one's grief: and if anyone judging my work is too hard-hearted for pity, he is welcome to assign the facts to the historical record, and the emotions to the historian.

[2.117–24, 162–66] The three types of Judaism, introduced in contrast to the doctrines of Judas of Galilee

Archelaus' territory was now designated a Roman province, and Coponius, a member of the equestrian order at Rome, was sent out as procurator with an authority from Caesar which extended to the death penalty. In his term of office a Galilaean called Judas incited his countrymen to revolt, preaching that it was cowardice to submit to Roman taxes and to tolerate mortal masters when God had been their only lord. This man was a preacher who started his own sect, and had nothing in common with the others.

Jewish doctrine in fact takes three forms. The adherents of these sects are called Pharisees, Sadducees, and, thirdly, Essenes.

The Essenes, who are native Jews, are particularly known for their high-minded discipline, and they are a closer-knit community than the others. They reject the pleasures of the flesh as vice, and see virtue in self-control and immunity to the passions. They disdain marriage for themselves, but take in other people's children when they are still innocent enough to be moulded by teaching, then treat them as their own family and imprint them with the moral character of the sect. It is not that they condemn marriage itself or its role in human propagation, but they believe that no woman stays faithful to any one man, and they want to keep themselves safe from female promiscuity. Wealth is of no interest to them, and they practise communism to a remarkable degree—you will not find any of them better provided than his fellows. It is their rule that new members admitted to the sect must surrender their property to the order, so that throughout the whole community neither abject poverty nor relative affluence is anywhere to be seen, but all individual possessions go into the common pool, and, like brothers, they all share in one household. They consider oil a defilement, and anyone accidentally smeared with it wipes his body clean, as their code requires a dry skin and white clothing at all times. Officers to run their community are elected by show of hands, and all have a vote in the allocation of their specific responsibilities. They are not based in any one city, but have large colonies throughout the country....

Of the two schools mentioned first, the Pharisees constitute the dominant sect, with a reputation for precise interpretation of the law. They attribute everything to Fate and to God: the choice of right or wrong action is largely up to men themselves, but they hold that Fate always takes a hand one way or the other. They believe that every soul is immortal, but only the souls of good people migrate to another body, while the souls of the unworthy are condemned to eternal punishment.

The Sadducees, the second of the orders, eliminate Fate altogether, and place God beyond any commission or sight of evil. They say that good and evil are there in the world for men to choose between them, and individual will determines which course to follow. They deny the permanence of the soul, and reject the notion of punishments in Hades or posthumous rewards.

The Pharisees show collegiate affection and promote harmonious relations with the general public, but the Sadducees behave rather uncivilly even to one another, and they take a snobbish approach to their fellow Jews, as if they were no better than foreigners. This, then, is what I have to say about the Jewish doctrinal schools.

[2.562–68] The appointment of Joseph son of Gorion and Joseph the son of Matthias (the historian) as generals to direct the revolt

When the Jews who had pursued Cestius returned to Jerusalem, they either forced or persuaded any remaining pro-Romans to join their movement, and held a mass meeting at the temple to appoint further generals to direct the war. Joseph the son of Gorion and Ananus the high priest were elected to absolute authority in all home affairs, with particular responsibility for raising the height of the city walls. Although Eleazar the son of Simon had his hands on the Roman booty, the money seized from Cestius, and the bulk of the public exchequer as well, they did not appoint him head of state, as they could see the potential despot in him, with his band of Zealots taking on the role of his enforcers. Gradually, though, the need for money and Eleazar's own skullduggery overcame the people's resistance, and they accepted him as supreme commander.

Two other generals were chosen for Idumaea, Jesus the son of Sapphas, one of the chief priests, and Eleazar the son of the high priest Neus: the existing governor of Idumaea, Niger (called 'the Peraean', as he came from Peraea, east of the Jordan), was instructed to take his orders from these generals. The rest of the country received no less attention. Joseph the son of Simon was sent to take command at Jericho, Manasseh in Peraea, and John the Essene in the toparchy of Thamna, with Lydda, Joppa, and Emmaus added to his area of responsibility. John the son of Ananias was appointed commanding officer of the districts of Gophna and Acrabata; and Josephus the son of Matthias was given both parts of Galilee, with his command extended to include Gamala, the strongest city in that region.

[3.379–408] *Josephus at Jotapata saves his own life and foretells that Vespasian will become emperor*

'Our best course then, my friends, is to take the sensible view and not compound our human predicament with impiety toward the God who created us. If our lives are to be saved, then let us save them: there is no disgrace in accepting life from those who have had such powerful proof of our courage in action. If we are to die, death at the hands of our conquerors is an honourable death. For my part, I shall never prove traitor to myself by going over to the enemy side. That would be yet more stupid than common desertion— deserters do it to save themselves, but for me it would be total destruction, a personal ruin. I hope, though, that the Romans are playing false. If they kill me after giving their word, I shall die happy—to find them faithless liars would be a vindication sweeter than outright victory'.

In these and similar terms Josephus argued long in an attempt to prevent the suicides. But desperation had blocked his fellows' ears, and they had long since consecrated themselves to death. He only succeeded in infuriating them. One after another they launched themselves at him, sword in hand, cursing him for a coward, and all of them were clearly ready to run him through there and then. By one means or another—a personal appeal, a straight glare of command, a hand grabbed, a disarming entreaty—and running the whole gamut of emotions in this crisis, he managed to keep all their swords from his throat, twisting and turning to face each new assailant like a cornered animal. As for them, even at this nadir of his fortune some respect for their commander still held: there was no strength in their thrusts, their blades glanced off him, and many came up with swords at the ready then instinctively dropped their points.

In this desperate situation his resource did not desert him. Putting his faith in God's protection, he took a gamble with his own life in making the following proposal: 'Look', he said, 'we are determined to die, so let's draw lots to decide the order in which each of us is killed by another—the man who draws the first lot is felled by the next in line, and so on through the whole group of us as fortune runs its course. That way no one will have to die by his own hand, and there will be nothing unfair—no one can change his mind and stay alive when the others are dead'. They thought this was a proposal made in good faith, so Josephus had his way and drew lots along with the others. As each man's lot came up, he presented his throat unhesitatingly for the next man to cut, confident that his commander would soon die likewise: the thought of a death shared with Josephus was sweeter than life itself. In the end there was only Josephus and one other man left (should we call this pure luck, or God's providence?). Keen to avoid either a death sentence dealt by the lot, or—if he was left till last—the need to pollute his hand with the blood of a fellow Jew, Josephus worked his persuasion on this man and came to a pact that they should both stay alive.

Having thus survived two wars—with the Romans and with his own people—Josephus was brought before

Vespasian by Nicanor. The Romans all flocked to see him, and there was a babel of noise from the crowd pressing in round the general—some whooping at the man's capture, others hurling curses at him, others forcing their way through for a closer look. Those at the back were clamouring for his execution as an enemy, while those nearer the front were more inclined to remember what he had once achieved and marvel at such a change of fortune. Among the officers there was not one who, whatever his earlier hostility, did not now relent at the sight of him. Titus in particular was powerfully affected by Josephus's resolute bearing in adversity and by pity for his youth. As he recalled the fighting man of just a few days ago, and saw him now helpless in the hands of his enemies, he had cause to reflect on the dominant role played by fortune, the quick turn of the scales of war, and the instability of all things human. So he was now instrumental in bringing most of the Romans round to sharing his own compassion for Josephus, and his was the voice which most influenced his father to save the prisoner's life. Even so, Vespasian had him kept in the strictest custody, with the intention of sending him straight on to Nero.

On hearing this, Josephus asked for a private audience with Vespasian. Vespasian had everyone else withdraw except his son Titus and two of his own close associates, and Josephus then began: 'Vespasian, you may think that in Josephus you have simply won yourself a prisoner of war: but I am come to tell you of your greater destiny. If I were not God's chosen emissary, I would have followed the Jewish tradition—I know it well, and how a defeated general should meet his death. Are you sending me to Nero? Why to him? Do you think Nero and his successors will last long before your hour is come? You, Vespasian, will be Caesar and emperor, both you and your son here with us. So chain me tighter now and keep me for yourself, as you, Caesar, are master not only of me but of all land and sea and the whole human race. Punish me, please, with yet harsher confinement if I am taking the name of God in vain'.

At the time Vespasian seemed unconvinced by this declaration, and supposed that Josephus was simply manoeuvring to save his life, but gradually he came round to believe it, as God was already prompting in him thoughts of empire and showing other signs predictive of the throne. And Vespasian discovered that Josephus had proved an accurate prophet in other matters also. One of the two associates present at the private meeting remarked that if Josephus's statement was not just a piece of nonsense designed to deflect the anger coming his way, it was surprising that he had not warned the people of Jotapata that their city would fall, or predicted his own captivity. Josephus replied that he had done both: he had told the Jotapatans that the city would be captured after forty-seven days, and had predicted that he himself would be taken alive by the Romans. Vespasian privately checked this with some of the other prisoners and found that it was true: this was when he began to take seriously what Josephus had told him about his own destiny. He still kept him chained and under guard, but supplied him with clothing and other luxuries, and always treated him with kindness and general consideration, a courtesy which had the active support of Titus.

[6.201–19] *Infant cannibalism at the height of the siege of Jerusalem*

There was a woman called Mary, daughter of Eleazar, who came from Transjordan, from the village of Bethezuba (which means 'House of Hyssop'). Hers was a distinguished and wealthy family, and she had fled with the rest of that population to Jerusalem, where like everyone else she had to suffer the siege. The warlords had robbed her of most of the possessions she had packed up and brought with her to the city from Peraea, and what was left of her treasures, together with any food she managed to procure, was carried off in the daily invasions of their henchmen. The poor woman conceived a furious resentment, and her constant abuse of the looters and the curses she called down on them only provoked them further. When no one was exasperated or pitying enough to kill her, when she was exhausted by her efforts to find food which others would then take—and wherever she looked it was now impossible to find any food—and when hunger was coursing through every organ and bone in her body, and anger burning her up yet more fiercely than hunger, she allowed fury to join necessity in steering her to an act against all nature. She laid hands on her own child, an infant still at the breast. 'Poor baby', she said to him, 'when all is war, famine, and party strife, should I keep you alive for any of these? With the Romans that means slavery, if we are still living when they come; but famine is faster on us than slavery, and the partisans are worse than either. So here we go: let's have you becoming food for me, an avenging ghost to haunt the partisans, and the one story the world still needs to complete the picture of Jewish suffering'. With that, she killed her son, roasted his body and ate half of it, then covered up and saved the rest.

The partisans were there in no time, caught the smell of the unspeakable roast, and threatened her with instant execution unless she produced the dish she had prepared. Saying that she had kept a good portion for them, she brought out the remains of her child. The immediate effect was a horrified stupefaction, and they stood there frozen at the sight. She went on: 'This is my own lawful child, and this is my own doing. So eat! I have already eaten. Don't let yourselves be weaker than a woman or softer than a mother. But if you come over all pious and reject this sacrifice of mine, then let's say I have done your eating for you, and what's left should stay with me'. That sent them trembling on their way. This was the only case where their courage failed them, reluctant though they were to concede even this food to the mother. But the whole city was immediately filled with the news of this abomination, and everyone, picturing the tragic scene in their mind's eye, felt a shiver as if they themselves had gone that far. The starving longed for death, and thought the lucky ones were those who had met their end before they had word or sight of such horrors.

News of this ghastly event soon reached the Romans. Some refused to believe it, others were moved by the pity of it, but the effect on most was to intensify their hatred of the whole Jewish people. Caesar once more declared before God that he was not responsible for this tragedy. He protested that he had offered the Jews peace, self-government, and an amnesty for all past offences, and they had deliberately chosen sedition rather than unity, war rather than peace, and famine when they could have enjoyed a plentiful prosperity; and they had started with their own hands the firing of the temple which they, the Romans, were trying to keep safe for them. So such hideous food was no more than they deserved. But he would bury the stain of this cannibal infanticide under the ruins of its country, and not leave on the face of the earth in the light of the sun a city in which mothers fed themselves like that. But it was the fathers, he said, not the mothers, who were responsible for the resort to such food: it was they who were obstinately remaining under arms even after privations as acute as these. In making this declaration of intent, Titus was equally conscious of the desperate state to which their opponents were reduced: they would never now come to a sensible agreement when all that could have changed their minds before it happened had already been visited on them.

[6.236–43] *Titus's council of war and the decision not to destroy the Temple*

On the next day Titus ordered a division of his army to extinguish the fire and level the approach to the gates so the legions would have an easier way up. He then called a meeting of his officers. Gathered first were his six most senior colleagues—Tiberius Alexander, the Camp Prefect; Sextus Cerealius, Larcius Lepidus, and Titus Phrygius, the commanders respectively of the Fifth, Tenth, and Fifteenth Legions; Haterius Fronto, the commander of the two legions from Alexandria; and Marcus Antonius Julianus, the procurator of Judaea. The other procurators and the tribunes were brought in next, and Titus raised for debate the question of the temple. Some took the view that the usual rule of war should be enforced, as there would be no end to Jewish revolts as long as the temple still stood as a rallying-point for Jews all over the world. Others recommended that the temple should be spared if the Jews evacuated it and left no armed presence, but if they used it as a platform for hostilities, it should be burnt: it would then be no longer a temple, but a fortress, and the consequence would not be any impiety by the Romans, but the impiety of those who had forced the Romans to take action. Titus replied that even if the Jews did use it as a platform for hostilities, he would not take vengeance on inanimate objects rather than men, and would never burn down a monument of such splendour: its loss would damage the Romans, just as its preservation would retain a jewel of the empire. Reassured to hear this, Fronto, Alexander, and Cerealius now happily expressed their concurrence with his view. So Titus then concluded the meeting, instructed the officers to stand down the rest of the troops, so he could have them reinvigorated when action resumed, and ordered the contingent of men already picked from the cohorts to create a road through the ruins and put out the fire.

[6.300–309] *The prophecy of Jesus son of Ananias about the destruction of Jerusalem*

More alarming still was what happened four years before the war, when all was peace and prosperity in the city. One Jesus, the son of Ananias, an ordinary farmworker, came to the feast at which it is the Jewish custom for everyone to erect a tabernacle for God. Inside the temple he suddenly began to cry out, 'A voice from the east, a voice from the west, a voice from the four winds, a voice against Jerusalem and the temple, a voice against bridegrooms and brides, a voice against the whole people'. Day and night he went round all the streets uttering this same cry. Some of the leading citizens took offence at his ill-omened rant, laid hold of the man, and subjected him to a severe beating. He stayed silent under the blows—not a word in his own defense or for the enlightenment of his assailants—and then continued to make the same proclamations as before. The magistrates, rightly supposing that there was something demonic driving the man on, brought him before the Roman procurator. There, though the whips were lacerating him to the bone, he made no plea for mercy and shed no tear, but with his voice pitched in the most sorrowful tone responded to each lash with 'Woe to Jerusalem!' When Albinus, the procurator, asked him who he was and where he came from, and why he was broadcasting this message, the man made no reply to any of his questions, but just kept on reiterating his lament for the city. In the end Albinus concluded that he was mad, and released him. In the whole period up to the outbreak of war he never accosted or was seen talking to any of the citizens, but every day, as if it was some mantra he had learnt by heart, he kept repeating the lament, 'Woe to Jerusalem!' Day after day, when people beat him, he did not curse them; when they offered him food he did not bless them; his only response to anyone was that dark foreboding. He was at his most vocal during the festivals. He kept this up, strong-voiced and tireless, for seven years and five months, until, after seeing what he had foreboded become a reality, he was finally silenced during the siege. He was going round on the wall shouting loud and clear, 'Woe again to the city, to its people, and to the temple', and as he added the coda, 'And woe to me too!' a stone shot from a catapult struck him and killed him instantly. So those forebodings were still on his lips when the life left him.

[7.96–99] *The sabbatical river*

Titus Caesar, as we have said, stayed for some time in Berytus. His onward journey from there took him through several cities in Syria, in each of which he put on lavish spectacles involving his Jewish prisoners in exhibitions of their own extermination. In the course of his travel he saw a river with properties which deserve mention. This river runs between Arcea, a part of Agrippa's kingdom, and Raphanaeae, and shows a remarkable peculiarity. When it flows, it is a full stream with a brisk current; but then it fails at source and for the space of six days gives no evidence other than a dry bed; and after that, as if there had been no intervening change, it pours out again in full flow on the seventh day just as before. It has always been observed to keep strictly to this timetable, which is why they call it the Sabbatical River, a name borrowed from the seventh day held sacred in the Jewish religion.

[7.375–406] *The speech of Eleazar son of Yair on suicide and the tragic end of the siege of Masada*

'Where now is that great city, the mother-city of the whole Jewish race, secure behind all those rings of walls, protected by all those guardposts and massive towers, with hardly enough room for its arsenal of munitions, and with all those tens of thousands of fighting men to defend it? Where has it gone, that city of ours which was believed to have God as its founder? It has been torn up by the roots and swept away. The only memorial left of it is the camp of those who destroyed it, still quartered in the ruins—that and some sad old men sitting by the ashes of the temple precinct, and a few women kept back by the enemy for the most abhorrent violation.

'Which of us with this picture in his mind will bear to look any longer on the light of the sun—even if he could live on in safety? Who is such an enemy to his country, such a coward, such a clinger to life, as not to regret that he is still alive today? If only we had all been dead before we had to see that holy city razed by enemy hands, that sacred temple so profaned and ripped from the ground! But since we nurtured a hope, noble enough in itself if deluded, that we could perhaps take vengeance for the city on its enemies, and now that hope is gone, leaving us exposed in an impossible situation, let us go straight for an honourable death, and do a kindness to ourselves, our children, and our wives while that kindness is still in our power. We were all born to die, as are those who have been born to us: and even the fortunate cannot escape death. Rape, enslavement, the sight of wives led off with their children to a degrading fate—these are not horrors somehow inherent in the human condition, but result from the cowardice of men who have the opportunity to forestall them by death, and refuse to take it. We were so proud of our courage when we revolted from the Romans, and now when it has all come to an end and they offered to save our lives, we rejected that offer. So can any of you fail to foresee the obvious effects of their fury if they take us alive? Pity the young men with the physical strength to sustain prolonged torture, and pity the men past their prime who are too old to survive the abuse. Are we going to have men seeing their wives roughly dragged away, and hearing their children cry "Daddy!" when their own hands are tied? No, as long as those hands are free and can hold a sword, let them do us honourable service. Let us die unenslaved by the enemy, and let us all, together with our children and wives, leave this life as free men. This is what our law prescribes, this is what our wives and children implore us to do. This is the compulsion which God has visited on us—and the outcome the Romans least want to see, anxious as they are that not one of us should die before we are captured. So let us go to it! Let us cheat the Romans of the satisfaction they hope to have from us, and leave them instead the shock of our death and amazement at our initiative'.

He would have prolonged his homily, but was cut short by his audience, all of them now filled with an overmastering urge to do the deed as quickly as could be. They rushed off like men possessed, each urgent to act faster than the next man, and thinking it would prove their courage and conviction if they were not seen to be among the last: such was the intensity of the passion which had seized them to slaughter their wives, their children, and themselves. You might have expected their resolution to falter when they faced the actual deed, but that was not so. They kept unwaveringly to the intention they had formed in the course of Eleazar's speech, and despite the warmth of family affection which was still strong in all of them, reason—that this was the best option for their loved ones—triumphed over emotion. As they clutched their wives in a final embrace, and took their children in their arms and clung to those last kisses, with their tears running, it was then that, as if hands other than their own were their agents, they carried through their purpose, with the thought of the horrors their families would otherwise suffer at the hands of the enemy providing a consoling justification for the need to kill them. In the end every one of them proved up to the enormity of what they had resolved, and all accounted for each member of their closest family, one after the other—poor wretched men, forced by necessity to decide that killing their own wives and children with their own hand was the lesser of two evils!

Unable to bear any longer their anguish at what they had done, and feeling that it would wrong the dead if they outlived them for more than a brief moment, they quickly piled all their possessions into one heap and set fire to it. Then, after choosing by lot ten of their number to be the executioners of the rest, each man flung himself down by his wife and children where they lay dead, took them in his arms, and offered his throat to those charged with this painful duty. They unflinchingly slaughtered them all, then set themselves the same lottery rule. Whoever drew the lot was to kill the other nine and himself last of all—such was their shared confidence that there was no difference in the way that any of them would either act or submit. So finally the nine presented their throats, and the one last survivor first checked that in the whole spread of bodies in this massive carnage there was no one still needing his hand to finish them: satisfied that all were dead, he set the palace ablaze, and then with all the force of his hand drove his sword right through his body, and fell dead alongside his family. These last died in the belief that they had left no animate being open to capture by the Romans. But in fact one old woman had managed to hide in the underground aqueducts which brought drinking water to the fort, and also another woman, a relative of Eleazar, in intelligence and education superior to most of her sex, together with her five children. They had concealed themselves there while the others were concentrating on the mass killings. The total number of the dead, including women and children, was 960. This tragedy was enacted on the fourteenth of the month Xanthicus.

Expecting further resistance, the Romans armed at dawn, laid gangways across from their earthworks to bridge the approach, and then launched their assault. Seeing no sign of the enemy, but only a weird emptiness wherever they looked, a fire burning further in, and total silence, they had no idea what could have happened. At length they raised their war cry, as if it was the signal to open fire, hoping that this would bring out someone from wherever they were inside. The two women heard their shout, and emerged from the underground conduits to tell the Romans what had taken place, the second woman giving a clear and comprehensive account of the speech proposing it and of the way in which the deed was carried out. They were reluctant to accept her story, and could not believe the enormity of such a resolve. They set to extinguishing the flames and soon had cut a path through them to get inside the palace. When they came on the mass of slaughtered bodies, there was none of the usual sense of triumph over an enemy: instead they could only feel a wondering admiration for the nobility of their collective decision and for the disregard of death which so many had resolutely taken to its conclusion.

Abbreviations Used in the Notes

AJ	*Jewish Antiquities*
b.	*Babylonian Talmud*
BJ	*Jewish War*
C.Ap	*Against Apion*
Companion	H. H. Chapman and Z. Rodgers, eds., *A Companion to Josephus* (Chichester, 2016)
JMJC	A Schatz, ed., *Josephus in Modern Jewish Culture* (Leiden, 2019)
Jos.	Josephus
JRA	*Josephus Reception Archive* (http://josephus.orinst.ox.ac.uk/archive)
RJEMP	M. Goodman and J. Weinberg, eds., Special Issue: 'The Reception of Josephus in the Early Modern Period', *International Journal of the Classical Tradition* 23 (2016)
Vita	*Life*

CHAPTER 1: BEGINNINGS

1. On the death of Agrippa I, see Jos. *AJ* 19.343–52; Acts 12:19–23; on Agrippa and Berenice in the *Jewish War*, see M. Goodman, 'The Shaping of Memory: Josephus on Agrippa II in Jerusalem', in G. J. Brooke and R. Smithuis, eds., *Jewish Education from Antiquity to the Middle Ages: Studies in Honour of Philip S. Alexander* (Leiden, 2017), 85–94.

2. Suetonius, *Divus Vespasianus* 5.6.

3. On Josephus in Jerusalem after the fall of the city, see Jos. *Vita* 417–21; on his life in Rome, see *Vita* 423–29.

4. On his invention of the term *theokratia*, see Jos. *C.Ap.* 2.165.

5. S. J. D. Cohen, *Josephus in Galilee and Rome: His Vita and Development as a Historian* (Leiden, 1979).

6. On Flavian propaganda about the defeat of the Jews, see F. Millar, 'Last Year in Jerusalem: Monuments of the Jewish War in Rome', in J. Edmondson, S. Mason, and J. B. Rives, eds., *Flavius Josephus and Flavian Rome* (Oxford, 2005), 101–28.

7. On Justus's history, see Jos. *Vita* 336–60.

8. Thucydides, *History of the War between Athens and Sparta* 1.1, 22; on Josephus in relation to Polybius, see A. M. Eckstein, 'Josephus and Polybius: A Reconsideration', *Classical Antiquity* 9.2 (1990), 175–208.

9. H. Chapman, 'What Josephus Sees: The Temple of Peace and the Jerusalem Temple as Spectacle in Text and Art', *Phoenix* 63 (2009), 107–30; Suetonius, *Divus Vespasianus* 5.6; Tacitus, *Historiae* 5.1–5; Cassius Dio, *Historia Romana* 66.1.4; Eusebius, *Historia Ecclesiastica* 3.9.2.

CHAPTER 2: EARLY YEARS (100–1450)

1. On the 'parting of the ways', see M. Goodman, 'Modeling the "Parting of the Ways"', in Goodman, *Judaism in the Roman World: Collected Essays* (Leiden, 2007), 175–85; Jesus's predictions of the destruction of the Temple in Mark 13:2; Matthew 23:38; 24:2; Luke 19:40–44; 21:6, 20–24. On the sufferings of the Jews as divine punishment, see, e.g., *BJ* 6.310; 7.34, 271.

2. Theophilus, *To Autolycus* 3.23; Minucius Felix, *Octavius* 33.4. See M. E. Hardwick, *Josephus as an Historical Source in Patristic Literature through Eusebius* (Atlanta, 1989).

3. Hippolytus, *Philosophoumena* 18–31.

4. *AJ* 18.63–4. The received text in the manuscripts reads, 'At that time there arose Jesus, a wise man, if indeed one should call him a man. For he was a performer of marvellous works,

a teacher of those who receive with pleasure the truth. And he won over many Jews and many of the Greeks. He was the Christ. When Pilate, upon hearing him accused by the foremost men among us, condemned him to the cross, those who first loved him did not cease. For he appeared to them on the third day alive again, the holy prophets having foretold these things and many other marvels about him. And even now the tribe of Christians, so called after him, has not disappeared'. It has long been recognized that the text has been corrupted by Christian additions, but the extent of the corruption has been debated since early modern times. See A. Whealey, *Josephus on Jesus: The Testimonium Flavianum Controversy from Late Antiquity to Modern Times* (New York, 2003); Jerome, *De Viris Illustribus* (PL 23, 629–31); *Homilia dicta tempore famis et siccitatis*; Basil, in *Patrologia Graeca* 31.324.

5. Eusebius, *Historia Ecclesiastica* 3.5, 6; see S. Inowlocki, 'Josephus and Patristic Literature', in *Companion*, 363.

6. Citation of Porphyry in Eusebius, *Praeparatio Evangelica* 9.3.1.

7. Cyril of Alexandria, *On Zechariah* 12.11–14; Melito, *Peri Pascha* 52; Jerome, *Epistulae* 22.35; Cassiodorus, *Institutiones* 1.17.1 (ed. Mynors, p. 55).

8. Cassiodorus, *loc. cit*; see D. B. Levenson and T. R. Martin, 'The Ancient Latin Translations of Josephus', in *Companion*, 323; on the origins of some Josephus translations in Constantinople, see C. M. Mazzuchi, 'Natura e storia del Guiseppe Flavio ambrosiano', in S. Costa and F. Gallo, eds., *Miscellanea Graecolatina*, vol. 4 (Rome, 2017), 271–318.

9. Ps.-Hegesippus, *De excidio urbis Hierosolymitanae* 1.1.8; 2.12 (citations of Josephus); 2.2 (Simon Magus); see K. M. Kletter, 'The Christian Reception of Josephus in Late Antiquity and the Middle Ages', in *Companion*, 368–82.

10. List of authors translated by Rufinus in Gennadius, *De Viris Illustribus* 17.

11. On Josephus's own claims about his Jewish readership, see Jos. *Vita* 362, 365; *C. Ap.* 1.51.

12. *Lamentations Rabbah* I: 5, no. 31; *b. Gittin* 56 a–b; on the parallels between Josephus and Yohanan and the different evaluation of Yohanan in rabbinic sources, see A. Tropper, 'Yohanan ben Zakkai, *Amicus Caesaris:* A Jewish Hero in Rabbinic Eyes', *JSIJ—Jewish Studies, an Internet Journal* 4 (2005), 133–49, with references to copious earlier studies.

13. On parallels between rabbinic texts and Josephus in general, see T. Ilan and V. Noam, 'Remnants of a Pharisaic Apologetic Source in Josephus and in the Babylonian Talmud', in M. Kister et al., eds., *Transmission and Transformation from Second Temple Literature through Judaism and Christianity in Late Antiquity* (Leiden, 2015), 112–33, with references to earlier studies; on 'causeless hatred', see b. *Yoma* 9b; on the transfer of stories from Palestine to Babylonia in the fourth century, see R. Kalmin, 'Josephus and Rabbinic Literature', in *Companion*, 295; on the adoption in Palestine of traditions in *Lamentations Rabbah* in response to Christian historiography, see H. Zellentin, 'Jerusalem Fell after Betar: The Christian Josephus and Rabbinic Memory', in R. Boustan et al., *Envisioning Judaism: Studies in Honour of Peter Schäfer on the Occasion of His Seventieth Birthday* (Tübingen, 2013), 1:319–67.

14. On the sources of *Sefer Yosippon*, see S. Dönitz, '*Sefer Yosippon (Josippon)*', in *Companion*, 385.

15. On attitudes toward suicide in *Sefer Yosippon*, see M. Hadas-Lebel, *Flavius Josephus: Eyewitness to Rome's First-Century Conquest of Judea* (New York, 1993), 230–31.

16. On Ibn Hazm and *Sefer Yosippon*, see D. Flusser in D. Flusser, ed., *Josippon [Josephus Gorionides]*, 2 vols. (Jerusalem, 1980), 2:11–12; on Mosconi, see A. Schatz, 'A Tradition in the Plural: Reframing *Sefer Yosippon*'s Josephus for Modern Times', in *JMJC*, 67.

17. On all these versions, see Dönitz, '*Sefer Yosippon (Josippon)*', 386–87.

18. On the Ibn Daud compilation, see K. Vehlow, ed., *Abraham Ibn Daud's Dorot Olam (Generations of the Ages)* (Leiden,

2013); on the Chronicles of Jerahme'el, see Bodleian Library Manuscript Hebrew d.11 in E. Yassif, ed., *The Book of Memory: That Is, The Chronicles of Jerahme'el* (Tel Aviv, 2001) (in Hebrew); on the influence of *Sefer Yosippon*, see Dönitz, '*Sefer Yosippon (Josippon)*', 384; on the attitude of Jews to historiography in general, see Y. H. Yerushalmi, *Zakhor: Jewish History and Jewish Memory* (Seattle, 1982).

19. Malalas, *Chronographia* 1.10 ('wise'); 10. 260 ('Hebrew present at the war'); *Chronicon Paschale* I, p. 463, 11.16–21 (on the destruction as punishment for the death of James).

20. R. Fishman-Duker, 'The Second Temple Period in Byzantine Chronicles', *Byzantion* 47 (1977), 126–56, provides a general overview. Her more detailed discussion specifically of Josephus's writings in these chronicles is forthcoming. On Josephus and Niketas Choniates, see A. Simpson, 'From the Workshop of Niketas Choniates: The Authority of Tradition and Literary Mimesis', in P. Armstrong, ed., *Authority in Byzantium* (Farnham, 2013), 263–64; T. Kampianaki, 'Preliminary Observations on the Reception of Flavius Josephus in Byzantine Historical Writings', *Byzantina Symmeikta* 28 (2018), 209–28.

21. Theodore Metochites, *Miscellanea* 15; on the papyrus fragment (P. Apion Graec. Vindobensis 29810, cf. R. A. Pack, *The Greek and Latin Literary Texts from Greco-Roman Egypt*, 2nd ed. [Ann Arbor, 1965], 74, no. 1283); see H. Schreckenberg, *Die Flavius-Josephus—Tradition in Antike und Mittelalter* (Leiden, 1972), 54–55; on the scribe of Barocci 151, see N. Wilson, 'Observations on the *editio princeps* and Two Neglected Manuscripts of the Greek Text', in *RJEMP*, 177.

22. On the Syriac manuscript, see S. P. Brock, 'Josephus', in S. P. Brock et al., eds., *Gorgias Encyclopedic Dictionary of the Syriac Heritage* (Piscataway, N.J., 2011), 232. An edition of the manuscript by David Taylor is forthcoming.

23. K. Leeming, 'The Slavonic Version of Josephus's *Jewish War*', in *Companion*, 390–401.

24. On the *Jewish War* in the Latin West, see Kletter, 'Christian Reception of Josephus in Late Antiquity'; on the medieval dramatic traditions, see S. K. Wright, *The Vengeance of Our Lord: Medieval Dramatizations of the Destruction of Jerusalem* (Toronto, 1989). A major research project at the University of Bern, with the title "'Lege Iosephum!' Ways of Reading Josephus in the Latin Middle Ages," will be devoted to the reception of the Latin Josephus.

25. For these specific images, see H. Schreckenberg, 'Josephus in Early Christian Literature and Medieval Christian Art', in H. Schreckenberg and K. Schubert, eds., *Jewish Historiography and Iconography in Early and Medieval Christianity* (Assen, 1992), 89, 92, 104, 106; on the medieval illustrations of manuscripts of Josephus more generally, see G. Deutsch, *Iconographie de l'Illustration de Flavius Josèphe au Temps de Jean Fouquet* (Leiden, 1986); U. Liebl, *Die illustrierten Flavius-Josephus-Handschriften des Hochmittelalters* (Frankfurt am Main, 1997).

26. H. Lewy, 'Josephus the Physician: A Medieval Legend of the Destruction of Jerusalem', *Journal of the Warburg and Courtauld Institute* 1 (1937–38), 221–42.

CHAPTER 3: REDISCOVERY OF THE GREEK BOOK (1450–1750)

1. D. Stein Kokin, 'The Josephan Renaissance: Flavius Josephus and His Writings in Italian Humanist Discourse', *Viator: Medieval and Renaissance Studies* 47.2 (2016), 205–48.

2. N. Wilson, 'Observations on the *editio princeps* and Two Neglected Manuscripts of the Greek Text', in *RJEMP*, 174.

3. Wilson, 'Observations on the *editio princeps*', 175, 179.

4. T. Roebuck, '"Great Expectation among the Learned": Edward Bernard's Josephus in Restoration Oxford', in *RJEMP*, 307–25.

5. Roebuck, 'Great Expectation', 317.

6. On the Spanish translations, see J. Weiss, 'Flavius Josephus, 1492', in *RJEMP*, 180; on France, P. M. Smith, 'The

Reception and Influence of Josephus's Jewish War in the Late French Renaissance with Special Reference to the Satyre Menippée', *Renaissance Studies* 13.2 (1999), 173–91; on the English translations of this period, G. Hata, 'A Note on English Translations of Josephus from Thomas Lodge to D.S. Margoliouth', in *Companion*, 414–18.

7. On W. Whiston, see J. E. Force, *William Whiston: Honest Newtonian* (Cambridge, 1985); M. Feingold, 'A Rake's Progress: William Whiston Reads Josephus', *Eighteenth-Century Studies* 49.1 (2015), 17–30; T. Rajak, *Josephus and Whiston* (Cambridge, Mass., forthcoming).

8. Sewel illustration in H. Schreckenberg, 'Josephus in Early Christian Literature and Medieval Christian Art', in H. Schreckenberg and K. Schubert, eds., *Jewish Historiography and Iconography in Early and Medieval Christianity* (Assen, 1992), 125; on illustrations of Josephus's works generally, see G. Huber-Rebenich, 'Illustrations of Printed Editions of Josephus in the Sixteenth Century', in *RJEMP*, 197.

9. On the Leipzig readings, see J. Eliot Gardiner, *Music in the Castle of Heaven: A Portrait of Johann Sebastian Bach* (London, 2013), 302; on Protestant readings of Josephus in England, see B. Groves, *The Destruction of Jerusalem in Early Modern English Literature* (Cambridge, 2015); on English playwrights, see P. Auger, 'Playing Josephus on the English stage', in *RJEMP*, 326–32.

10. Auger, 'Playing Josephus', 331.

11. On Münster's edition, see S. Dönitz, '*Sefer Yosippon (Josippon)*', in *Companion*, 386.

12. On Casaubon, see A. Grafton and W. Sherman, 'In the Margins of Josephus: Two Ways of Reading', in *RJEMP*, 231–32.

13. On the relationship of Josephus's Essenes to arguments about the origins of monasticism, see J. Machielsen, 'Sacrificing Josephus to Save Philo: Cesare Baronio and the Jewish Origins of Christian Monasticism', in *RJEMP*, 240; on the enthusiasm of Casaubon, see Grafton and Sherman, 'In the Margins', 234; on Scaliger, see C. P. E. Nothaft, 'Josephus

and New Testament Chronology in the Work of Joseph Scaliger', in *RJEMP*, 249.

14. W. Hayley and W. Cowper, *The Life and Letters of William Cowper*, 4 vols. (Chichester, 1809), 2:148–50 (Letter 39); on translations, see Hata, 'Note in English Translations', 416.

15. J. Weinberg, 'Early Modern Jewish Readers of Josephus', in *RJEMP*, 275, 277.

16. On Abravanel, see M. Avioz, 'Allusions to Josephus in Abravanel's Writings' (unpublished paper, Oxford, January 2013); on the *Sefer Yosippon* in Yiddish, see A. Schatz, 'A Tradition in the Plural: Reframing *Sefer Yosippon*'s Josephus for Modern Times', in *JMJC*, 66.

17. B. Wallet, 'Hidden Polemic: Josephus's Work in the Historical Writings of Jacques Basnage and Menahem Alexander', in *JMJC*, 42, 48–49, 52.

18. Wallet, 'Hidden Polemic', 47–57; letter of Menasseh ben Israel in Chr. Arnold, *XXX Epistolae Philologicae et Historicae de Flavii Josephi Testimonio* (1661), 163–65. It is not clear to which passages in book 7 of the *Jewish War* Menasseh was referring.

19. Schatz, 'Tradition in the Plural', 62–84, with Amelander citation quoted on 70.

20. Jos. *C. Ap.* 2.165.

21. J. Abolafia, 'Spinoza, Josephism and the Critique of the Hebrew Republic', *History of Political Thought* 35 (2014), 295–316.

22. See Y. Kaplan et al., eds., *Menasseh ben Israel and His World* (Leiden, 1989).

23. On uniformity of belief and practice within Judaism, see Jos. *C. Ap.* 2. 179–81; on Baronio, see Machielsen, 'Sacrificing Josephus to save Philo', 241–42; Uriel da Costa, *Examination of Pharisaic Traditions (Exame das tradições phariseas)*, trans. H. P. Salomon and I. S. D. Sassoon (Leiden, 1993).

CHAPTER 4: CONTROVERSY

1. E. Reuss, 'Josephus (Flavius)', in *Allgemeine Encyclopädie* 31 (Leipzig, 1855), 104–16, with citation from 107. I owe this reference to Marcus Pyka. On Reuss, see S. J. D. Cohen,

Josephus in Galilee and Rome: His Vita and Development as a Historian (Leiden, 1979), 11.

2. On Josephus in *HaMe'assef*, see Y. Cohen, 'The "Maskil Hero": The Image of Josephus in the Worldview of the Jewish Enlightenment', in *JMJC*, 94; on Grace Aguilar, see T. Rajak in *JRA*.

3. On Shalom haKohen, see Cohen, 'The "Maskil Hero"', 97; on Josephus in the *Jewish Chronicle*, see S. Pearce, 'Josephus and the *Jewish Chronicle*: 1841–1855', in *JMJC*, 106–43, with quote from 'Hertz ben Pinchas' on 139–40.

4. On Josephus in the Haskalah, see Cohen, 'The "Maskil Hero"', 94–104; on Lessing, see L. Hecht in *JRA*.

5. On Osiris, see D. Jarrassé, *Osiris: mécène Juif et nationaliste francais* (Le Kremlin-Bicêtre, 2009).

6. Pyka, 'In the Shadow of Napoleon: The Reception of Josephus between Jost, Salvador, and Graetz', in *JMJC*, 187–93.

7. Pyka, 'Shadow of Napoleon', 194–201.

8. Cohen, *Josephus in Galilee and Rome*, 11–13; D. R. Schwartz in *JRA*.

9. On the school prospectus, see J. Prager, 'Über das Verhältniss des Flavius Josephus, zur Zelotenpartei beim Ausbruch des Jüdischen Krieges', in *Jahresberich über die Religions-Unterrichts-Anstalt der Synagogen-Gemeinde* (Breslau, 1873), 3–10. I owe this reference to Danny Schwartz.

10. Pearce, 'Josephus and the *Jewish Chronicle*', 106, 165–66; on references from the *Jewish Chronicle* in the early twentieth century, see 'I. A.' [Israel Abrahams] on 22 March 1907; 'H. L.' [Herbert Loewe] on 30 April 1915, in a review of N. Bentwich, *Josephus* (Philadelphia, 1914); A. Cohen on 23 September 1921. I owe these references to Sarah Pearce.

11. On the trials of Josephus, see M. Hadas-Lebel, *Flavius Josephus: Eyewitness to Rome's First-Century Conquest of Judea* (New York, 1993), 237 (Antwerp); S. Sznol, 'Reading and Interpreting Flavius Josephus in the Vilna and Warsaw Ghettos (1941–1943)', in *JMJC*, 337–38 (Vilna); P. Vidal-Naquet, *Flavius Josèphe ou du bon usage de la trahison* (Paris,

1977), 34; A. Margalit, 'Josephus v. Jeremiah: The Difference between Historian and Prophet', *Biblical Archaeology Review* 38.5 (2012), 53–57; S. Avineri, 'Josephus the Zionist', *Haaretz*, 24 February 2011 (English ed.); Hadas-Lebel, *Flavius Josephus*, 237 (television program); on road names, see E. Ben Eliyahu, in *JRA* and M. Azaryahu, *Namesakes: History and Politics of Street Naming in Israel* (Jerusalem, 2012) (in Hebrew).

12. A. Zirkle, 'Dismantling Orientalist Fantasies and Protestant Hegemony: German Jewish Exegetes and Their Retrieval of Josephus the Jew', in *JMJC*, 218–19.

13. On the continuations of Josephus's histories in English publications, see O. Murray, 'The Western Futures of Ancient History', in A. Lianeri, ed., *Future Time in and through Greek Historiography* (Berlin, 2016), 381–94, with discussion of the summary histories of the Jews after Josephus included by Maynard and Bradshaw in their rival translations of Josephus in the 1790s as well as the much fuller sequels printed in the Whiston editions from ca. 1848 to ca. 1878; for the references in novels, see T. Hardy, *The Mayor of Casterbridge* (Auckland, 1886), 86; R. Kipling, *Captains Courageous* (New York, 1897), 48; M. Twain, *Roughing It* (Hartford, Conn., 1872), 168 [chap. 22]; L. Wallace, *Lew Wallace: An Autobiography* (New York, 1906), 2:891.

14. Pyka, 'Shadow of Napoleon', 187–93.

15. Zirkle, 'Dismantling Orientalist Fantasies', 232; Zunz letter of 25 February 1847 cited in N. N. Glatzer, ed., *Leopold and Adelheid Zunz: An Account in Letters, 1815–1885* (London, 1958), no. 262, p. 181.

16. On Halevy, see E. Sariel, 'Can't Live with Him, Can't Live without Him: Josephus in the Orthodox Historiography of Isaac Halevy and Ze'ev Yavetz', in *JMJC*, 242–49.

17. Citations all from Sariel, 'Can't Live with Him', 246–49.

18. For the attitude of the Hafetz Hayyim, see Sariel, 'Can't Live with Him', 242n6; on Yavetz, 249–60.

19. On Yavetz in relation to Halevy, see Sariel, 'Can't Live with Him', 260–63.

20. S. Feiner, 'Kalman Schulman's Josephus and the Counter-history of the Haskalah', in *JMJC*, 145, 147.

21. Feiner, 'Kalman Schulman's Josephus', 147–52.

22. L. Kahn, 'Kalman Schulman's Hebrew Translation of Jose-phus's *Jewish War*', in *JMJC*, 155–56.

23. Kahn, 'Kalman Schulman's Hebrew Translation', 155–84. Daniel Schwartz has pointed out to me that a further ex-planation may be the ease of reference to Josephus's book in footnotes, since the Hebrew word for 'wars' in the plural can stand alone in the construct form unlike the word for 'war' in the singular.

24. Feiner, 'Kalman Schulman's Josephus', 149.

25. On *HaMaggid*, see Cohen, 'The "Maskil Hero"', 85; on Loewisohn, see Pyka, 'Shadow of Napoleon', 150; on Levinsohn, see Cohen, 'The "Maskil Hero"', 95–97.

26. On Masliansky, see T. Rajak, 'Josephus through the Eyes of Zvi Hirsch Masliansky (1856–1943): Between Eastern Europe, the USA and Eretz Yisra'el', in *JMJC*, 264–80.

27. On Simchoni, see Kahn, 'Kalman Schulman's Hebrew Translation', 182–83.

28. D. R. Schwartz, 'From Masada to Jotapata: On Josephus in Twentieth-Century Hebrew Scholarship', in *Companion*, 420–22.

29. Schwartz, 'From Masada to Jotapata', 426–27.

30. I owe this information on Menahem Stern having first read Josephus as a child in Schulman's translation to Shmuel Feiner (pers. comm.); on Ben Zion Wacholder having begun to read *Sefer* Yosippon at the age of five, see S. Bowman, 'Yosippon and Jewish Nationalism', *Proceedings of the American Academy for Jewish Research* 61 (1995), 47n47.

31. On Amelander and *Sefer Yosippon*, see A. Schatz, 'A Tradi-tion in the Plural: Re-framing *Sefer Yosippon*'s Josephus for Modern Times', in *JMJC*, 83–84.

32. On Lamdan's poem and *Sefer Yosippon*, see Y. S. Feldman, '"The Final Battle" or "A Burnt Offering?": Lamdan's Masada revisited', *AJS Perspectives* (Spring 2009), 30–32.

33. On the manifesto proclaimed by Abba Kovner, see D. Porat, *The Fall of a Sparrow: The Life and Times of Abba Kovner* (Stanford, Calif., 2009), 71. The image of sheep being slaughtered might also, of course, have referred more generally to biblical images of sacrifice, such as Isaiah 53:7.

34. On Berdyczewski, see O. Scharf, 'Taking Josephus Personally: The Curious Case of Emanuel bin Gorion', in *JMJC*, 283–85.

35. Scharf, 'Taking Josephus Personally', 285–86.

36. Scharf, 'Taking Josephus Personally', 303–4.

37. J. N. Simchoni, 'Introduction' to Yosef ben Mattityahu, *Toledot milhemet ha-yehudim im ha-Romaim* (Warsaw, 1923), 40.

38. On Feuchtwanger, see Y. S. Feldman, '"Flavius" on Trial in Mandate Palestine, 1932–1945: Natan Bistritsky's Hebrew Play and Lion Feuchtwanger's German Trilogy', in *JMJC*, 318–28.

39. Feldman, '"Flavius" on Trial', 319–20.

40. Feldman, '"Flavius" on Trial', 327.

41. On the Yiddish Art Theater production, see J. Bloom, *JRA*, s.v. 'Josephus on Stage in New York (1933)'; on Bistritsky, see Feldman, '"Flavius" on Trial', 312–18.

42. B. Krupnik in *Haaretz*, 4 April 1941.

43. S. Sznol, *JRA*, s.v. 'Itzhak Katzenelson (1886–1944)'.

44. On Judith Montefiore, see T. Rajak, *JRA*, s.v. 'Judith Montefiore'.

45. E. Ben Eliyahu, *JRA*, s.v. 'Masada'.

46. A. Mashiach, 'The Ethos of Masada in Halakhic Literature', *Review of Rabbinic Judaism* 19 (2016), 68; see T. Rajak, 'Josephus, Jewish Resistance and the Masada Myth', in J. J. Collins and J. G. Manning, eds., *Revolt and Resistance in the Ancient World: In the Crucible of Empire* (Leiden, 2016), 219–33, and, more generally, on national Israeli myths about Masada, see Y. Zerubavel, *Recovered Roots: Collective*

Memory and the Making of Israeli National Tradition (Chicago, 1995), chap. 5.

47. Translation by Eyal Ben Eliyahu and Zur Shalev of Y. Shalev, 'Yosefus' in Y. Shalev, *Latur Aharei Ishah* (Tel Aviv, 1987), 80.

EPILOGUE: THE PRESENT AND FUTURE
OF THE *JEWISH WAR*

1. Obituary of Pierre Vidal-Naquet by O. Murray, *Independent*, 3 August 2006.

2. On the expanding horizons of Roman history, see for instance the inaugural lecture of Fergus Millar as Camden Professor in Oxford in 1986 (F. Millar, 'Empire, Community and Culture in the Roman Near East: Greeks, Syrians, Jews and Arabs', *Journal of Jewish Studies* 38.2 [1987], 143–64); L. H. Feldman, *Josephus and Modern Scholarship 1937–1980* (1984): L. H. Feldman, *Josephus: A Supplementary Bibliography* (New York, 1986). All current scholarship on Josephus and the reception of his works is profoundly indebted to Heinz Schreckenberg's fundamental studies in the 1960s and 1970s: H. Schreckenberg, *Bibliographie zu Flavius Josephus* (Brill, 1968); *Die Flavius-Josephus—Tradition in Antike und Mittelalter* (Leiden, 1972); *Rezeptiongeschichtliche und textkritische Untersuchungen zu Flavius Josephus* (Leiden, 1977).

3. S. Mason, 'Jews, Judaeans, Judaizing, Judaism: Problems of Categorization in Ancient History', *Journal for the Study of Judaism* 38.4 (2007), 457–512; J. J. Price in L. Ullmann, trans., *Toldot milhemet hayehudim baRoma'im* (Jerusalem, 2009), 23 (in Hebrew).

4. F. Raphael, *A Jew among Romans: The Life and Legacy of Flavius Josephus* (New York, 2013); A. Hoffman, *The Dovekeepers* (London, 2011).

5. A. Gitai, *La guerre des Fils de Lumière contre les Fils des Ténébres*, Ager Films video cassette (1993).

FURTHER READING

On Josephus in General

Bilde, P. *Flavius Josephus between Jerusalem and Rome: His Life,
    His Works and Their Importance.* Sheffield, 1988.

Edmondson, J., S. Mason, and J. Rives, eds. *Flavius Josephus and
    Flavian Rome.* Oxford, 2005.

den Hollander, W. *Josephus, the Emperors and the City of Rome.*
    Leiden, 2014.

Mason, S., ed. *Understanding Josephus: Seven Perspectives.* Sheffield,
    1998.

Rajak, T. *Josephus: The Historian and His Society.* 2nd ed. London,
    2002.

Thackeray, H. St. John. *Josephus: The Man and the Historian.* New
    York, 1929.

On the Jewish Revolt against Rome

Goodman, M. *Rome and Jerusalem: The Clash of Ancient Civiliza-
    tions.* London, 2007.

———. *The Ruling Class of Judaea: The Origins of the Jewish
    Revolt against Rome, AD 66–70.* Cambridge, 1987.

Mason, S. *A History of the Jewish War, AD 66–74.* Cambridge,
    2016.

Price, J. J. *Jerusalem under Siege: The Collapse of the Jewish State,
    66–70 CE.* Leiden, 1992.

Rhoads, D. M. *Israel in Revolution, 6–74 CE: A Political History
    Based on the Writings of Josephus.* Philadelphia, 1976.

Schürer, E. *The History of the Jewish People in the Age of Jesus
    Christ.* Rev. and ed. G. Vermes and F. Millar. Vol. 1. Edin-
    burgh, 1973.

On the Jewish War

Hammond, M., trans. Josephus. *The Jewish War*. Introduction and notes by M. Goodman. Oxford, 2017.

Mason, S. *Flavius Josephus: Translation and Commentary, Volume 1b: Judean War 2*. Leiden, 2008.

Thackeray, H. St. John. *Josephus: Vol. 2 (The Jewish War, Books I–II); Vol. 3 (The Jewish War, Books III–IV); Vol. 4 (The Jewish War, Books V–VII)*. Cambridge, Mass., and London, 1927–28.

Williamson, G. A., trans. *Josephus, The Jewish War*. Rev., with introduction and notes by E. M. Smallwood. London, 1970.

On Josephus as Historian of the Jewish War

Cohen, S. J. D. *Josephus in Galilee and Rome: His Vita and Development as a Historian*. Leiden, 1979.

Rodgers, Z., ed., *Making History: Josephus and Historical Method*. Leiden, 2006.

On the Reception of the Jewish War

Chapman, H. H., and Z. Rodgers, eds. *A Companion to Josephus*. Chichester, 2016, 305–454.

Goodman, M., and J. Weinberg, eds. *The Reception of Josephus in the Early Modern Period*. Vol. 23 of *International Journal of the Classical Tradition*. Berlin, 2016.

Schatz, A., ed. *Josephus in Modern Jewish Culture*. Leiden, 2019.

The Josephus Reception Archive (JRA), an online platform consisting of entries that provide brief introductions to individuals, works, places, and themes relating to the reception of Josephus, can be accessed at http://josephus.orinst.ox.ac.uk/archive.